IMAGES
of America

MARBLE FALLS

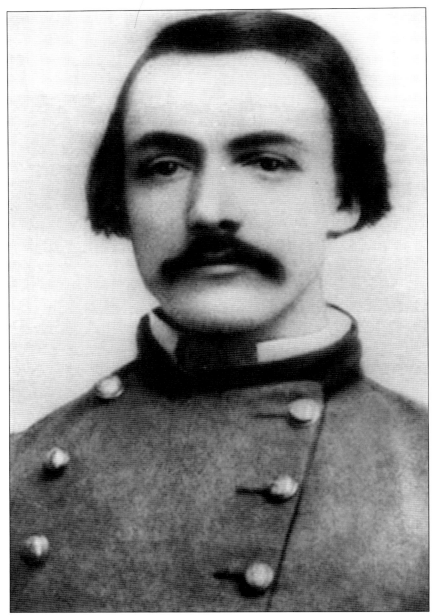

Adam Rankin Johnson, who moved from Kentucky to Burnet, Texas, in 1854, had visited the falls on the Colorado River while working as a surveyor in Texas. He returned to the South in 1861 to wear the uniform of the Confederacy. After the Civil War, the blind war veteran returned to Burnet County. In 1887, he and his business partners founded the town of Marble Falls in southern Burnet County. (Courtesy Burnet County Historical Society.)

ON THE COVER: Young people enjoyed boating at the falls as the 20th century opened. These well-dressed boaters took along an umbrella as well as three musical instruments. Although the falls were not actually marble, town founder Adam R. Johnson chose *Marble Falls* as the name for his 1887 town on the Colorado. (Courtesy Falls on the Colorado Museum.)

CONTENTS

Acknowledgments   6

Introduction   7

1.   First Settlers of Southern Burnet County   9

2.   Granite Mountain and Marble Falls   27

3.   Main Street   59

4.   Schools and Churches of Marble Falls   89

5.   Marble Falls in the 21st Century   103

6.   Historic Communities near Marble Falls   119

Bibliography   127

ACKNOWLEDGMENTS

Sincere thanks go to Marble Falls Library director Mary Jackson, along with Karen Davis and all other library employees; Fran McSpadden at the Falls on the Colorado Museum in Marble Falls; JoAnn Myers at the Herman Brown Free Library in Burnet; and Carole Goble, author and Burnet County Heritage Society board officer at Fort Croghan.

Ann Darragh, Caryl Calsyn, Milli Williams, and members of the Variegated Threads Quilting Bee gave encouragement for completion of the work, as did many members of early families as they made photographs available.

The historical collections and resources in Burnet County libraries, the Falls on the Colorado Museum in Marble Falls, and the Fort Croghan Museum in Burnet continuously served the needs of the authors. Many local history documents that were used have been preserved through efforts of the Burnet County Historical Commission; Burnet County Genealogical Society; Daughters of the Republic of Texas, Jane Wells Woods Chapter; and United Daughters of the Confederacy, Adam R. Johnson Chapter 2498.

Names of individuals who contributed images to the book are indicated. The following abbreviations are used to indicate sources of some photographs: Herman Brown Free Library (HB), Burnet County Heritage Society (BCHS), and the Falls on the Colorado Museum (FOCM). If no other indicator is given, the Marble Falls Library is the source of photographs.

Sites that have been awarded official markers by the Texas Historical Commission are indicated with (Texas Historical Marker).

INTRODUCTION

The ledges of the 22-foot-deep and 250-foot-wide natural falls now lie beneath lake water at Marble Falls, Texas. In the centuries before Marble Falls was founded on the Colorado River in 1887, the sound of the "great falls" on the Colorado attracted innumerable travelers, including various Indian tribes. Comanches were the final representatives of Native Americans in Central Texas.

A short distance to the west stood another landmark, a great 866-foot dome of solid pink granite that has been quarried and diminished in height since 1885.

In July 2012, Marble Falls celebrated the 125th anniversary of its founding. To mark the occasion, the Falls on the Colorado Museum Board sponsored a two-day event at the City Pavilion. Included among the guests were descendants of Gen. Adam Rankin Johnson, who is generally credited with founding the town of Marble Falls. Buddy Inman and other members of the Sons of the Republic of Texas fired several volleys of cannon shots out across the Colorado River in celebration.

Set in Burnet County in the Texas Hill Country within easy driving distance of the cities of Austin and San Antonio, today's Marble Falls has more than 7,500 residents. Nearby, Meadowlakes has 2,000 residents. Horseshoe Bay, where development began after 1970, numbers over 5,000. Marble Falls businesses busily serve 30,000 in a 10-mile radius of the town. The Scott & White Hospital complex that is developing five miles south of Marble Falls will add more to the population numbers.

The building of five dams and lakes—including Lake Marble Falls completed above Max Starcke Dam in 1951—prevented seasonal flooding on the Colorado River and helped the area become today's important retirement location and tourist destination. A new bridge has replaced the 1935 structure, and a new visitors' center stands at the north end of the bridge.

More hotels have opened in Marble Falls in recent years, and a good variety of restaurants and shops are available on Main Street, on US Highway 281, and on Ranch Road 1431. The Blue Bonnet Café has continued to serve pie and other good food since 1929.

Burnet County organized on August 7, 1854, soon after early resident Noah Smithwick attended an event in the falls area. He later recalled, "Barbecues were a feature of all political gatherings, the most notable one in that part of the country being given at the Marble Falls on the Fourth of July, 1854, prior to which time only the sound of the water leaping down the successive steps or benches that form the falls, and the voices of occasional small parties that had visited the spot, had awakened the echoes of the surrounding hills."

According to Smithwick, with no cannon available as they would be in 2012, the first number on the program that day in 1854 was a national salute fired from holes drilled in the rock. A lone fiddler played patriotic tunes, and Smithwick's son read the Declaration of Independence. An orator spoke at length before it was time for the meal to be served. At the end of the day, the fiddler provided music for dancing. Smithwick described the day as "the greatest event the country had every enjoyed." Some participants remained at the site for several days "to live it all over again."

Burnet County settlers, like residents of a number of West Texas counties, voted against secession when the Civil War loomed on the horizon in 1860. The threat of Indian raids, along with the heavy work of daily survival, undoubtedly influenced that vote. Also, newly-arrived county residents from Europe did not want secession. However, the statewide vote carried Texas into the Confederate States of America. Some Burnet County men were assigned to protect the home front or to provide agricultural products for the Confederacy. Others, like Adam R. Johnson, went to the battlefront.

Johnson was born in Henderson, Kentucky, in 1834 and moved to Burnet, Texas, in 1854, just as Burnet County was organizing. The young man soon gained a fine reputation as a surveyor and as an Indian fighter in his new location.

Johnson married Josephine Eastland in Burnet on January 1, 1861. With the outbreak of the Civil War on February 4, 1861, he returned to Kentucky and enlisted as a scout under Nathan Bedford Forrest. His subsequent exploits as commander of the Texas Partisan Rangers within the federal lines in Kentucky earned him a colonel's commission in 1862 and a promotion to brigadier general in 1864.

One of his most remarkable feats was the capture of Newburgh, Indiana, from a sizable Union garrison. Johnson had only 12 men and used two joints of stovepipe mounted on the running gear of an abandoned wagon to confuse his enemy and win the battle.

Later, Johnson was blinded and captured at an 1864 skirmish in Kentucky. Upon his release and the end of the war, he returned to Burnet County, where he lived for his remaining 60 years and became a community leader and a successful businessman. In January 1874, he joined others at the Austin capitol to help end Reconstruction for Texas by removing Gov. E.J. Davis from office and installing Richard Coke as the duly elected governor.

The Burnet County population in the 1880s had grown to 6,855, and citizens had begun to recover from the war and the Reconstruction years that followed. Because the time was right, Johnson was able to find others who were willing to invest in founding Marble Falls, "the blind man's town."

Since Marble Falls was developed in an organized manner, photographic images are available of many activities from its early times. The first granite school and some of the first homes and other structures still exist and play a part in the modern town. Several of these buildings have been awarded official Texas Historical Commission markers. In addition, the Roper Hotel is listed in the National Register of Historic Places.

Marble Falls serves as a kind of business hub for a number of surrounding communities. These communities also are an important part of this history and have been included in this book to help preserve the legacy of the whole Marble Falls area.

It is hoped that this work will be of use to longtime residents who would like a quick reference to their town's history. Hopefully, it also will offer the historical reference needed by new residents and visitors, especially those who may be new to Texas.

One

First Settlers of Southern Burnet County

Native Americans in Central Texas were gradually replaced by Anglo and German Americans and blacks from eastern Texas counties. Only a few Hispanic settlers came to the area before modern times.

Packsaddle Mountain, a Llano County mountain that can be seen on the southwestern horizon from Marble Falls, was the site of the last local battle between the white settlers and Comanche Indians. According to the Texas Historical Marker, the battle was fought August 4, 1873, when Capt. J.R. Moss and seven other men "routed a band of Indians thrice their number."

Many early settlers of Central Texas previously had been Texians, residents of the Republic of Texas (1836–1845). After Texas became the 28th state in 1845, more settlers risked the dangers of life on the Texas frontier as they moved northwest, up the Colorado River. They helped with the organization of Burnet County in 1854.

The families of Samuel Holland and Jesse Burnam were the first major land investors in Burnet County. Today, those early families, along with descendants of Rev. Adolfus Fuchs and others, continue to be well represented in the Marble Falls area.

During the 1860s, county residents focused on surviving daily threats of frontier life as well as the effects of the Civil War. Following the war, Texans suffered the aftermath of the conflict for more than a decade.

Burnet residents included a young, wounded Confederate veteran named Adam Rankin Johnson. Despite having been blinded in a Kentucky battle, Johnson returned to Texas to support his family in Burnet. His trips through the Colorado River area continued to reinforce his idea that a settlement should develop near the falls on the Colorado.

Charles S. Todd purchased land and sold several lots for a town in 1854, but his plans did not work. A post office was opened south of the river in 1884, and other investors tried and failed to develop settlements. It was Adam Rankin Johnson and his partners who successfully founded a town, Marble Falls, in 1887.

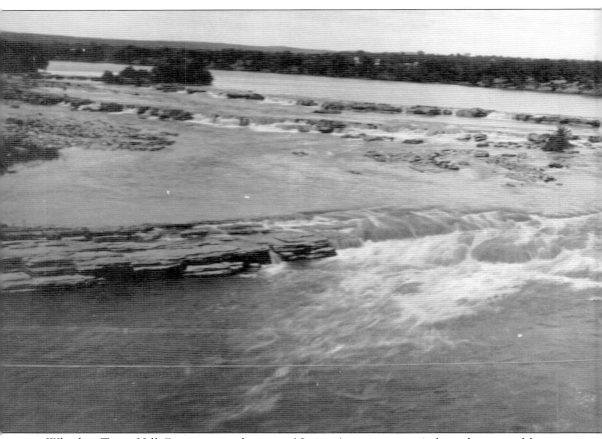

Whether Texas Hill Country travelers were Native Americans or settlers who arrived later, they turned toward the magnificent marble-like falls that Smithwick described as "the ceaseless roar of the splendid volume of water, dashing and leaping from ledge to ledge." Land developers recognized the possibility of the immense power for moving mills and serving the needs of man. Sometimes, the area of the falls made it easier for travelers to cross the Colorado River and to

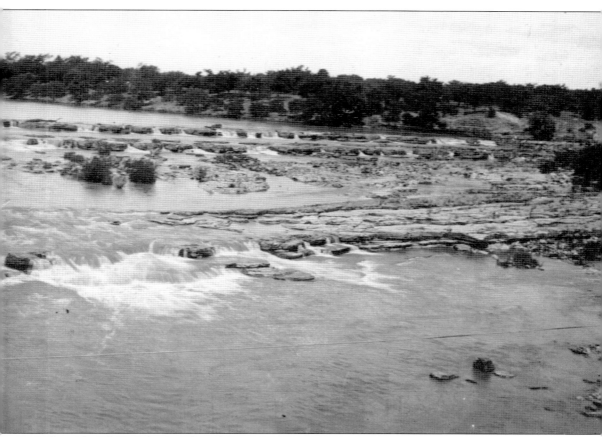

drive their livestock toward market. But in times of river flooding, the need for a ferry boat or a bridge was great. Some ferry service became available even before the first bridge was built in 1891. In addition, engineers made several attempts to build dams that would control the devastating effects of river flooding.

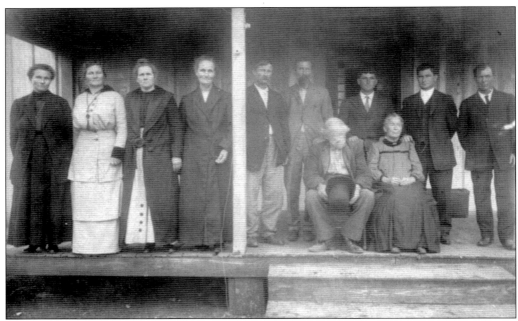

Samuel Ely Holland (1826–1917) is shown in his later years with his family at their home in Hamilton Valley. In 1848, after serving with Jack Hays's Texas volunteers, Holland became the first permanent area settler when he purchased 1,280 acres on Hamilton Creek, south of present-day Burnet. Fort Croghan was established the year after Holland built his log cabin. Holland, an Indian fighter in the early days, became a community leader and then served in the Texas legislature in 1897. His first son, George A. Holland, in 1853 became the first white child born in Burnet County, as is noted on his gravestone located in Holland Cemetery off Mormon Mill Road. Samuel continued buying land and became the largest landowner in the county. Many Holland descendants presently live along Mormon Mill Road, which runs north from Marble Falls. (Elaine Holland Turner.)

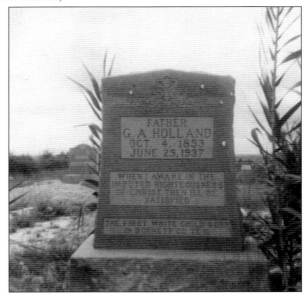

David Benjamin Holland (1856–1926), son of S.E. and Clara Thomas Holland, is shown with his son Marshall Holland (1881–1947). Marshall's mother was Lucy Holland. The family's property included a small marble quarry, and a block of this marble was hauled by oxcart to Austin, then shipped by rail to Washington, DC, as the Texas contribution to the Washington Monument, completed in 1888. (Elaine Holland Turner.)

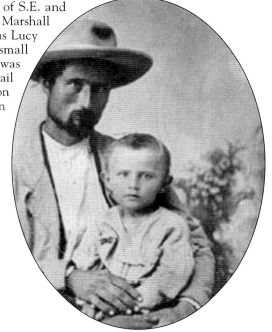

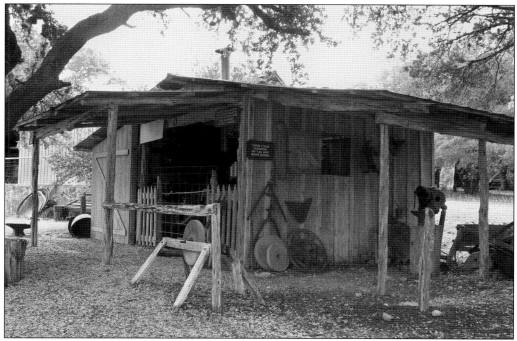

The Holland/Smithwick blacksmith shop is pictured as it is preserved at Fort Croghan in Burnet. A sign explains the purpose of such a shop: "Horses had to be shod, wagons mended, branding irons made, news exchanged, and a few tall tales told." S.E. Holland cultivated the first farm in Burnet County and built the first all-stone house for a home. He and Peter Kerr may have brought the first white-faced cattle. (Cristy Bromley.)

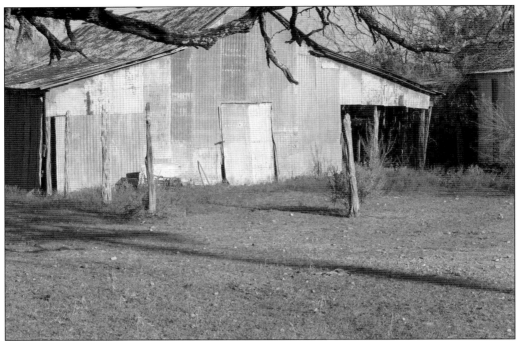

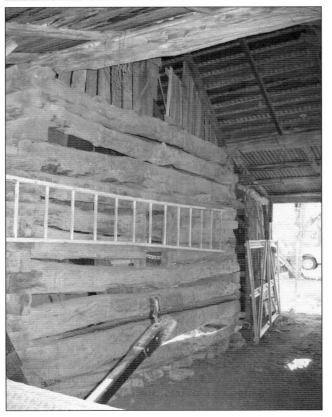

Jesse Burnam, who joined Stephen F. Austin's Old 300 Colony in 1821, played an important role during the Texas Revolution for independence from Mexico in 1836. After Texas became a state in 1847, two of Jesse's sons, William and Robert Thompson Burnam, moved northward up the Colorado River from their former home near LaGrange, Texas. In the 1850s, Jesse and his second wife, Nancy, moved also, arriving in time to help organize Burnet County. With land bought south of the Colorado River, Burnam became the second-largest landholder in the county. Pictured here is the large log cabin he built for his family near Double Horn Creek. External and interior views of the structure show its large size and the kind of logs that Burnam brought from his former location, Burnam's Ferry, near LaGrange.

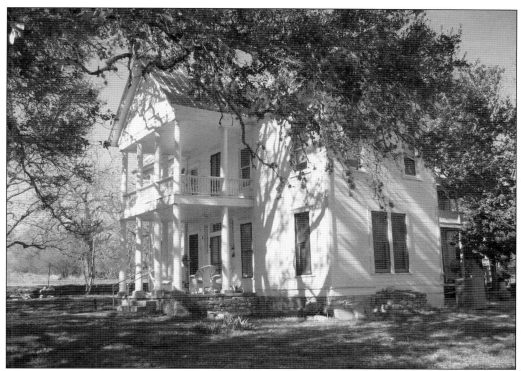

After Jesse Burnam built the back section of the larger home shown here, his first, log home was used as a barn. All structures and a nearby springhouse are still in use by the family. After a life of service to family and community, Jesse Burnam died in 1883 and was buried in the Burnam cemetery near his home. The engraving on his tombstone reads, "He whose merit deserves a temple has scarcely found a grave in the annals of Texas history."

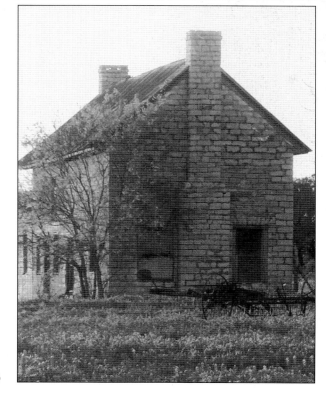

Now in ruins and located on US Highway 281, north of Marble Falls, the stone house pictured here was a popular subject for photographers and artists when bluebonnets were in bloom. Christian Dorbandt, who had been a soldier at Fort Croghan, built the first of three sections of the house in 1853. Later, Logan Vandeveer's daughter Elisa Hubbard lived there. Her son Peter is buried in a small cemetery nearby. (BCHS.)

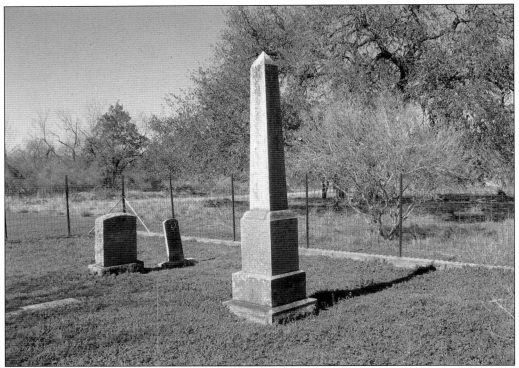

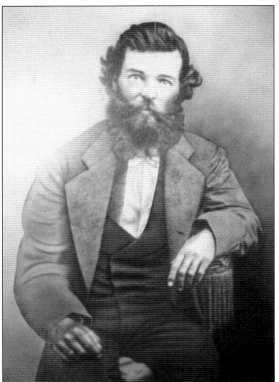

Rev. Adolphus Fuchs, his wife, Luise, and seven children came from Germany to Texas in 1846, hoping for better religious, cultural, and economic opportunities. With help from surveyor Jacob de Cordova in 1853, they moved to their land grant on the south banks of the Colorado River in the area now known as Cottonwood Shores. Pictured here, the graves of Adolphus and Luise Fuchs and other family members are found in the Fuchs Cemetery in that village. The first burial in the cemetery was Ino Fuchs Varnhagen in 1869. Though Reverend Fuchs never served as a Lutheran pastor in Texas, he taught music and officiated at the marriages of his children and those of other German families in the area. Conrad Fuchs, pictured at left, was the couple's oldest son and was buried here after his death in 1898. (Texas Historical Marker.) (FOCM.)

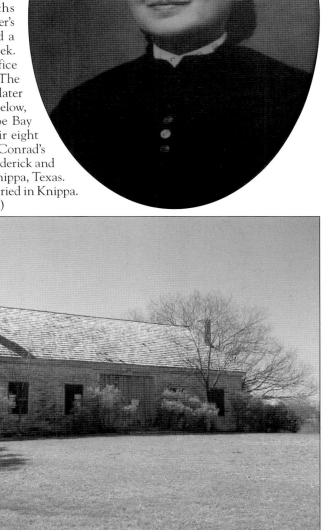

Pictured at right is Anna Perlitz Fuchs, who married Reverend Fuchs's son Conrad. Anna and Conrad Fuchs bought 160 acres southwest of his father's property. There, Conrad operated a steam mill at the head of Tiger Creek. Tiger Mill was designated a post office in 1872, with Conrad as postmaster. The family lived first in a log cabin and later in the spacious rock home pictured below, which is now part of the Horseshoe Bay development. The first two of their eight children died of diphtheria. After Conrad's death in 1898, Anna and her son Frederick and daughter Lina moved to a farm in Knippa, Texas. Anna Fuchs died in 1923 and was buried in Knippa. (Texas Historical Marker.) (FOCM.)

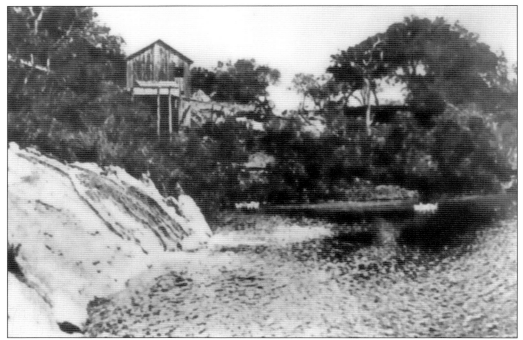

Mormon Mill Road in Marble Falls leads north to the location of the waterfalls on Hamilton Creek shown here. Mormon Lyman Wight and 150 followers left Illinois in 1844. After trying other locations in Texas, they settled near the waterfalls in 1851 and remained two years. Using waterpower, they set up a grain mill and a furniture factory to serve settlers. (Texas Historical Marker) (BCHS.)

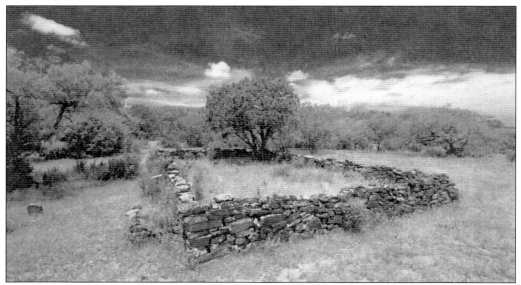

A number of Mormons became active in their new community and helped the citizens of Hamilton petition the state legislature to create Burnet County. On a hill overlooking the mill, this cemetery is all that is left of the Mormon settlement. Some Mormon families later lived briefly in the Double Horn area of Burnet County before moving on to Bandera County. (HB.)

After the Mormons moved away from Hamilton Creek in 1853, the mill was owned and operated at various times by Noah Smithwick, Samuel Ely Holland, and others. A post office was established in 1856, and the public school pictured here remained open in the community through the 1940s. The area retains the name of Mormon Mill. The waterfalls are located on private ranchland. (Beulah Holland.)

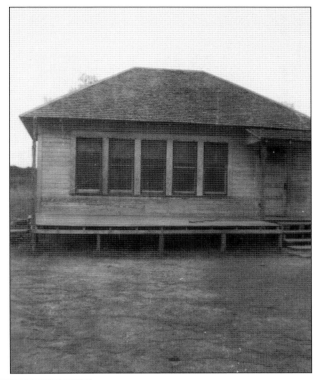

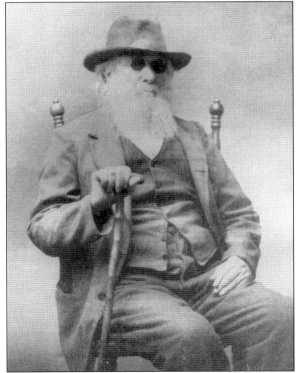

Noah Smithwick (1808–1899) moved from Tennessee to Texas in 1827. He participated in the Texas Revolution, then served as a Texas Ranger. He worked as the armorer at Fort Croghan in 1849 and later bought Mormon Mill. The community of Smithwick was named for him. In 1861, he moved to California rather than serve the Confederacy. In later years, he published memoirs of his life in Texas, including his time in Burnet County. (HB.)

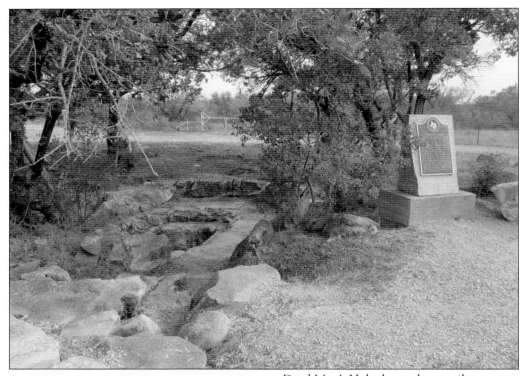

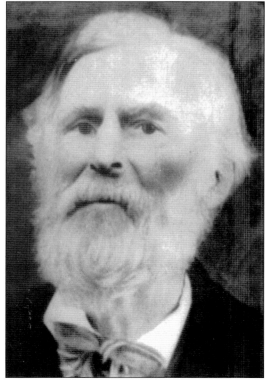

Dead Man's Hole, located two miles south of Marble Falls, was recorded by entomologist Ferdinand Lueders in 1821. During the Civil War era of the 1860s, it became the dumping ground for up to 17 bodies, including those of pro-Union judge John R. Scott and settlers Adolph Hoppe and Ben McKeever. An oak tree that once stood over the cave was said to have rope marks caused by hangings. (Texas Historical Marker.)

Edward Ebeling arrived in Texas from Germany in 1858. He began buying land on the south side of the Colorado River in 1859, paying 25¢ per acre. During the Civil War, he did not serve as a soldier but as a supplier of horses, mules, and other necessities for the Confederacy. He was a rancher but also became a banker in Marble Falls. (Deanna Bradshaw.)

In 1903, Hulda Giesecke married Rudolph Ebeling, son of Edward and Christiana Fissler Ebeling. Daughter Frances Dorchester taught in Marble Falls before moving to Galveston. Daughter Helen married Don H. Cude, who was school superintendent of Marble Falls from 1927 to 1941. Daughter Nookie worked at Barnes Lumber Company in Marble Falls. (Deanna Bradshaw.)

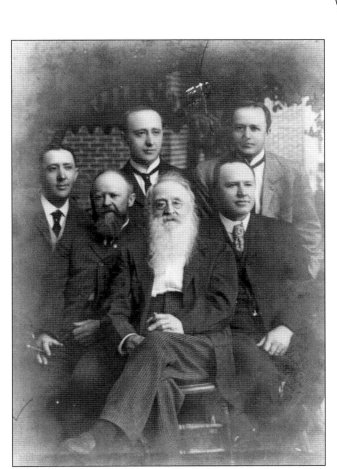

This image shows Albert Giesecke with his sons. Pictured are, from left to right (first row, seated) Ernst, Walter, Albert (father), and Paul Giesecke; (second row, standing) Max and Albert (son) Giesecke. The elder Albert came with his parents to Texas in 1846. After 1865, he moved with his wife, Ottilie Fissler Giesecke, and family to sections of land he had bought near Shovel Mountain in Burnet County. The first post office for Shovel Mountain was established in the Giesecke home in 1869. (HB.)

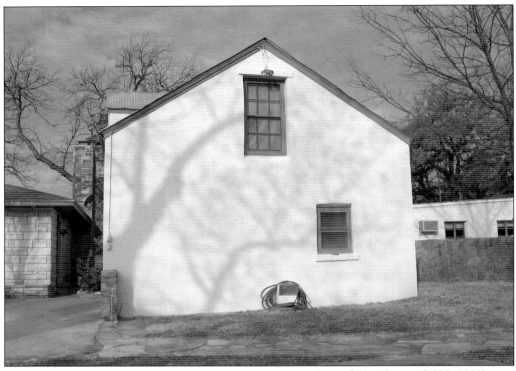

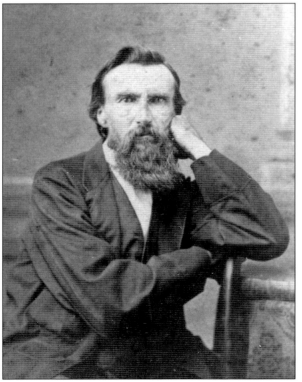

Amand Von Struve (1838–1902) came to Texas in 1848 with his father, a former Imperial Russian officer. Amand bought 8,000 acres south of the Colorado River in 1858 and added herds of horses, cattle, and sheep. He added this stone springhouse and kitchen in 1869 to protect food and water from roving Indians and animals. He married Christiana Fissler Ebeling in 1871. (Texas Historical Marker.)

Rudolf Richter moved with his wife, Wilhelmine Schroeter Richter, and their family from Germany to Texas in 1855, seeking more freedom. In 1861, Richter bought property from Adolph Hoppe in Burnet County south of the Colorado River. Richter served as postmaster of Double Horn, with the post office in his home from 1866 to 1882. The Richter children studied at home until rural schools were built. (HB.)

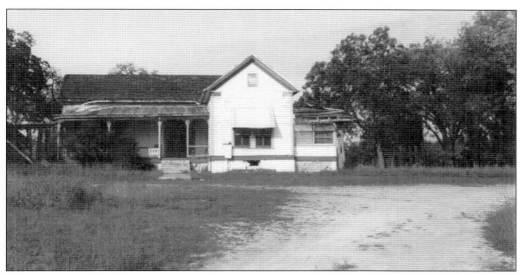

After their marriage in 1886, Ivo B. and Mina Kellersberger Matern owned this ranch house that was located in present-day Horseshoe Bay until it was removed in 2011. The Materns bought the George Christian home in Marble Falls in 1908 for use when their five children were in school, but the family returned to this ranch home when school was not in session.

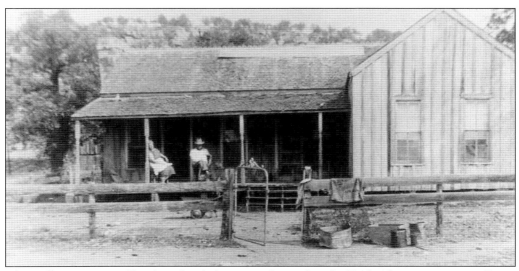

The William Ransom Slaughter family home was located in the Fairland community, northwest of Marble Falls. A nearby ridge is called Slaughter Mountain, and a cemetery also carries the family name. Ransom and his brother George Webb Slaughter settled on a land grant of over 4,000 acres that their father, William Slaughter, had received for his services to the Republic of Texas. (HB.)

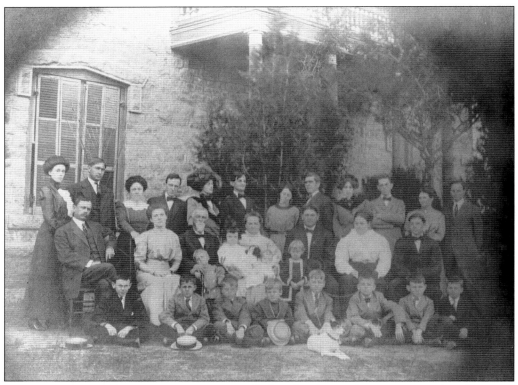

Badger family members are pictured at the Adam R. Johnson home named Rocky Rest, set on Hamilton Creek in Burnet. Like Johnson, Brandt Badger was a Confederate veteran. He moved from Gonzales to Burnet in 1885 and soon afterward joined Johnson in founding Marble Falls. The Johnson family moved from this location after the construction of their second home, Airy Mount. (BCHS.)

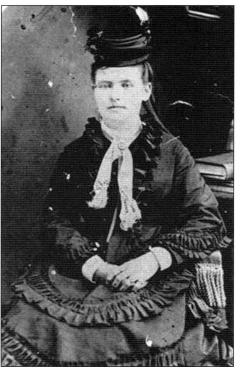

Adam R. Johnson married Maria Josephine Eastland in Burnet in 1861 before leaving to serve in the Confederate army. After the war, the Johnsons became parents of nine children, three of whom died young while the family lived at Rocky Rest. Johnson died in 1922, and his wife, in 1923. Both are buried in the Texas State Cemetery in Austin. (BCHS.)

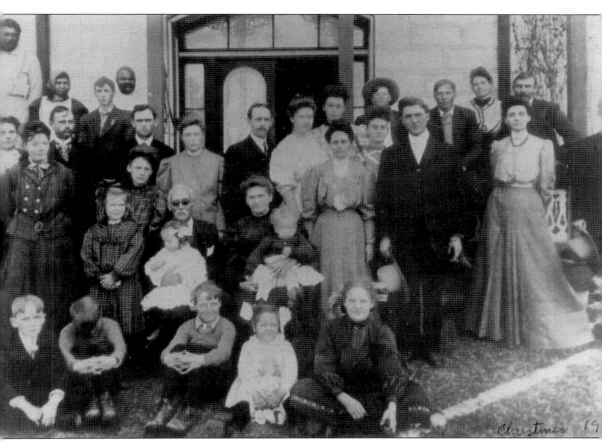

Christmas 19

Adam R. Johnson and his family are pictured at Christmas 1906 in front of their second home, Airy Mount, built in 1884. The Johnsons chose to build on a hill overlooking Burnet because they thought their living at Rocky Rest on Hamilton Creek had caused their children's illnesses. The new home was constructed of rock from a nearby quarry and lumber brought by oxcart from Bastrop. Soon after the home was in use, Johnson and his business partners sold the first lots in the new town of Marble Falls. Some family members made Marble Falls their home, while others remained in Burnet. Johnson and his wife enjoyed a long and happy life of more than 60 years together. After 1923, the property fell into disrepair but later was restored by Charles and Roseann Hayman, who converted the barn into a bed-and-breakfast inn. (Texas Historical Marker) (BCHS.)

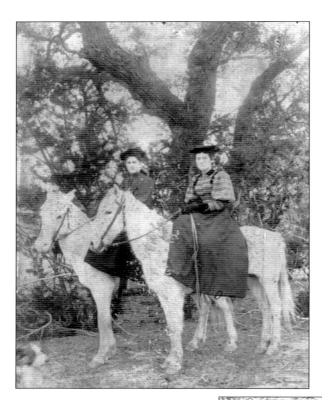

Women needed horseback-riding skills in the 19th century in the Colorado River country of Texas. At a time when stylish dress for ladies required hats and gloves, these two unidentified women rode sidesaddle, as was the custom required of women.

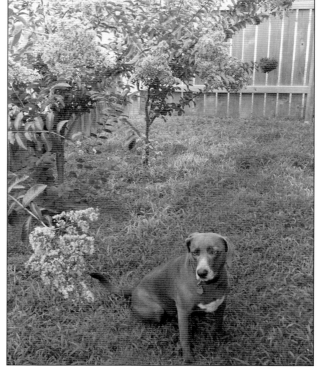

The Blue Lacy was declared the official dog breed of Texas in 2005. The beginnings of the breed date to 1858, when the Lacy brothers moved from Kentucky to the Granite Mountain area before the founding of Marble Falls. The breed is a mix of greyhound, scent hound, and coyote or wolf and was bred to herd cattle or hogs to market. Pictured is nine-year-old Cody, a Blue Lacy now retired in Burnet.

Two

Granite Mountain and Marble Falls

When Adam R. Johnson and his partners chartered the Texas Mining & Improvement Company in 1887, the time was right to found a town. People wanted to move to the area, and the national economy was beginning to recover from the stress of the Civil War. Johnson's partners included his son R.E. Johnson; nephew Adam Rankin of Kentucky; T.E. Hammond, C.T. Dalton, W.H. Roper, and F.H. Holloway, all of Burnet County; B. Badger of Gonzales County; and sons-in-law W.H. Badger and George Christian.

The company opened sales of Marble Falls town lots on July 12, 1887. The Bertram newspaper editor wrote, "The sale of town lots will commence at 10 o'clock in the morning at the grand stand, which is situated on the hill about the center of town." An Austin newspaper later reported a count of "3,000 people on the ground" that day to spend $30,000 on lots ranging in price from $75 to $750. The new town benefitted from its proximity to the river, which offered a water source for settlers and water power for industrial use, and to Granite Mountain, which offered building materials.

Heirs of William Slaughter were the first owners of Granite Mountain, located a few miles west of the future site of Marble Falls. The mountain property came to them as part of a 4,000-acre land grant from the Republic of Texas.

Confederate veteran George W. Lacy and his brother Frank Lacy bought the mountain for $3,453 in 1867. The George W. Lacy family set up housekeeping nearby, where they raised their 10 children.

Lacy worked with Johnson and his partners to develop a contract with the state of Texas. Under the agreement, the state built a railroad from Burnet to Granite Mountain in exchange for free pink granite to build the present state capitol, completed in 1888. After that contract using convict labor was completed, the mountain provided work for residents of the area. More than a century later, it continues to be of importance for its granite and for local employment.

In the 1890s, Thomas Darragh came from New York to purchase the mountain for $100,000. The Darragh family owned the property until the 1950s, when they sold it to Cold Spring Granite of Minnesota.

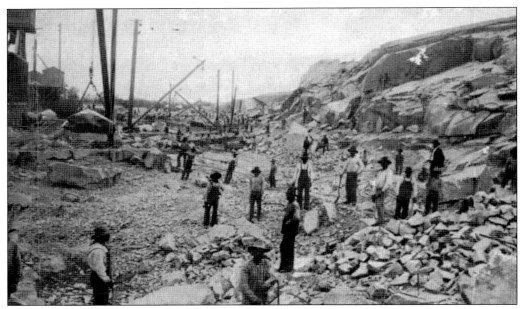

Adam R. Johnson, along with Confederate veterans and mountain owners George W. Lacy, Dr. W.H. Westfall, and N.L. Norton, worked with state leaders on an agreement to exchange granite for a 16-mile railroad extension from Burnet to the mountain. In order to cut costs, the legislature voted to use convict labor at the mountain in 1885, as shown in this image. (Mary Lucas.)

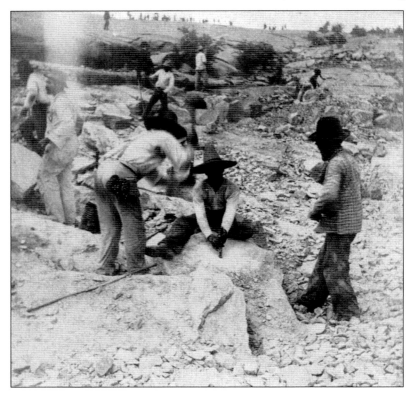

Convicts are pictured in 1885 at work on Granite Mountain, west of the future site of Marble Falls. The *Burnet Bulletin* reported 64 men in the first group of convicts from Huntsville, including whites, Mexicans, and blacks. A later report gave the numbers as 200 convicts in quarrying and 100 in cutting the stone. Abner Taylor supervised the laborers, and Gus Wilke was the stone contractor.

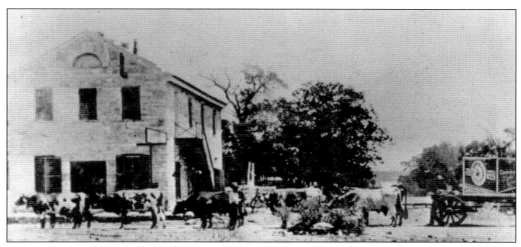

Before a railroad was built to the mountain in 1885, wagonloads of granite were moved by ox teams. The oxen and wagon pictured were on Main Street, on their way to the Burnet depot. Johnson had been instrumental in bringing rail service to Burnet in 1882. (BCHS.)

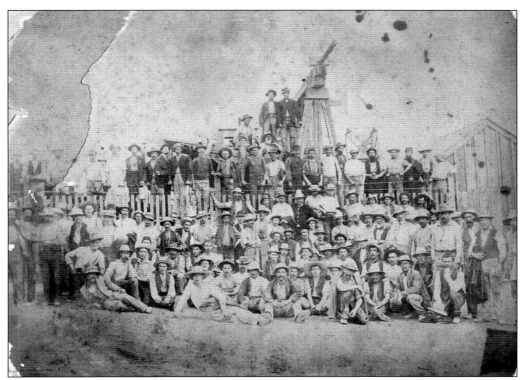

Because the American stone builders' union boycotted the convict project, Gus Wilke brought 62 stonemasons from Scotland to cut the stone. Although it was said that he broke the law by hiring convicts, he continued to use convict labor at the quarry and on the capitol building until the Austin structure was completed in 1888. (BCHS.)

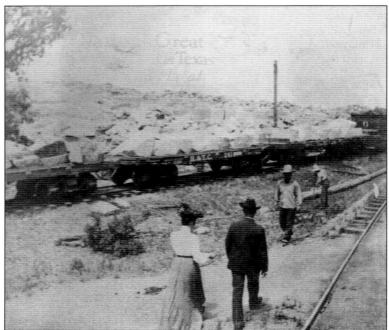

A woman dressed in the styles of the 1880s is shown walking with her escort along the railroad track near Granite Mountain, probably before the tracks were extended into Marble Falls in 1889. Tracks were built from Burnet to the Fairland depot and then on to the mountain by 1885, at a cost of $58,000. More than 15,700 carloads of granite had been sent to Austin by 1887.

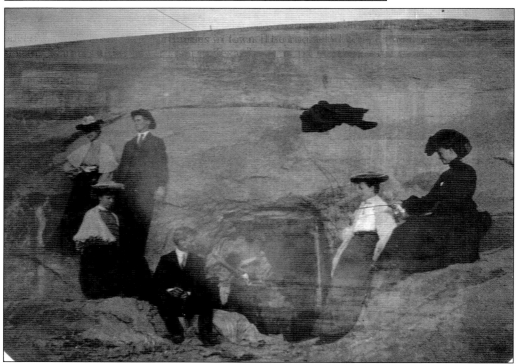

When young people in Marble Falls had spare time, they often chose a trip to Granite Mountain for an outing. These well-dressed men and women are shown visiting the entrance to a mountain cave where the original convict workers were locked in at night until 1888, when granite shipments for the Texas capitol were completed.

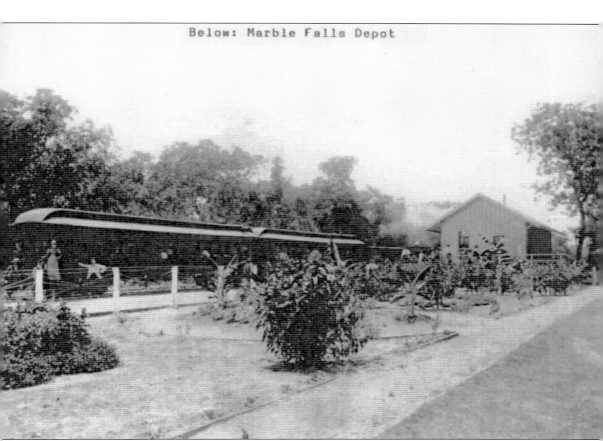

The Marble Falls train depot was built in 1889 near Second Street and Avenue N, a location that could be considered the town's first "main" street. Passengers boarded the train there, and livestock and local products could be loaded from stockyards built behind the depot. The first year's shipments included 4,600 loads of granite, 31 cars of hogs, 33 cars of horses and cattle, 144 cars of cedar wood and posts, 6 cars of pecans, 3 cars of hides, and 1,210 bales of cotton. George Lacy often sent four carloads of hogs by rail to market. In earlier times, the hogs lost weight when they were driven overland by Lacy hog dogs and their handlers. In 1923, a group of 2,800 turkeys were driven on foot from Round Mountain across the bridge over the Colorado River. They spent the night roosting in the factory building and, the next day, were driven to the depot and loaded on the train in time to get to market for Thanksgiving. (HB.)

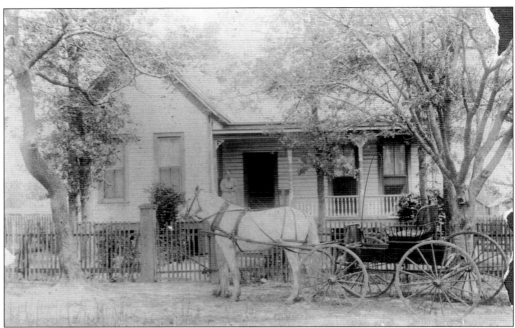

The depot was such an important location in early Marble Falls that people soon began to build houses and businesses nearby. Pictured are two of a number of homes that were built. People often gathered to see who was arriving or departing on the train or to enjoy the park built next to the station. As late as 1936, a group of 34 Spicewood citizens traveled by train to the Centennial Exposition in Dallas. With its wooden benches and potbellied stove surrounded by a large box of sand for the benefit of the tobacco chewers, the depot was used until 1960. Then, flooding from the river caused business owners to move to the higher ridge that is today's Main Street. The depot was remodeled in 1976 and moved to US Highway 281, where it was used as a chamber of commerce visitors' center until 2013. (Texas Historical Marker.)

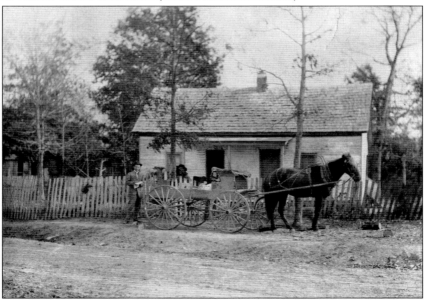

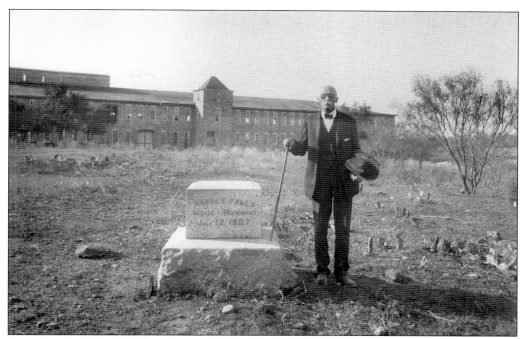

Town founder Adam R. Johnson is pictured in later years with a granite marker inscribed, "Marble Falls, Initial Monument, July 12, 1887." An arrow cut into the top of the marker helped surveyors lay out the town. Johnson never let blindness keep him from leadership roles. In 1922, the funeral for the well-known leader was held in the senate chamber of the capitol. He and his wife were buried in the Texas State Cemetery in Austin.

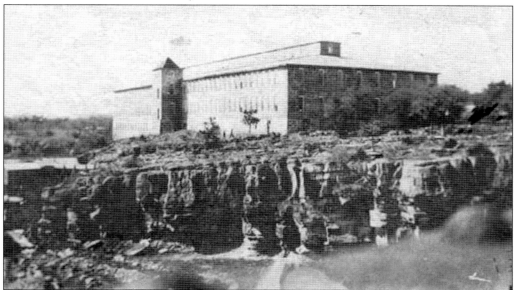

The falls had the potential for providing waterpower for a mill, and southern Burnet County produced cotton that could be sent to a mill. These two facts led to the formation of the Farmers Alliance with local farmers. Adam R. Johnson and other area leaders organized the Marble Falls Cotton & Woolen Co. in 1892 to build a factory with an adjacent powerhouse. (HB.)

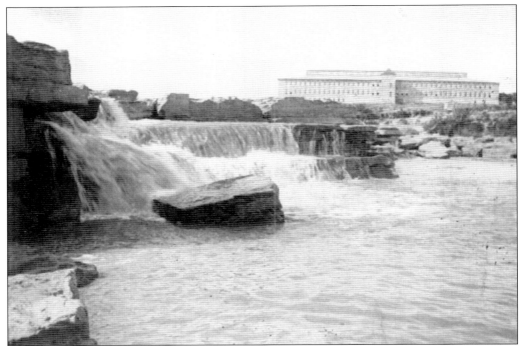

The factory was built of stone and was two stories tall, 100 feet wide, and 300 feet long, diagonal to the Colorado River bridge. From the beginning, the factory had problems. It was too close to the river and flooded easily, and its basement was too small to house the necessary machinery. It was seldom used for its original purpose. (Jean Eades.)

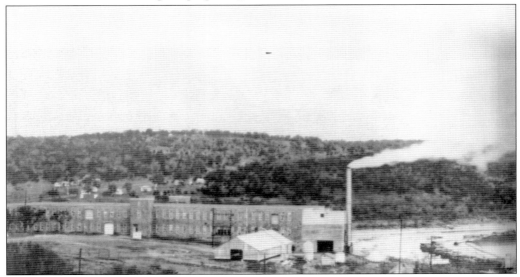

The north side of the factory is pictured along with a view of houses built on the south side of the Colorado River. In 1924, investors from Delaware bought the factory and built a retention dam across the river to compound water and produce electric power. Limited use of the factory followed until 1964, when the building burned. The area remained unused until 1998, when it was cleared to make way for a Hampton Inn and restaurants. (Jean Eades.)

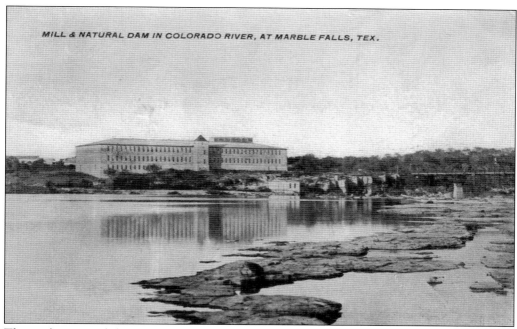

MILL & NATURAL DAM IN COLORADO RIVER, AT MARBLE FALLS, TEX.

This early postcard shows the factory and its improved powerhouse, with the first Marble Falls bridge pictured east of the factory. In its later years, before it burned in 1964, the factory building was used for a variety of businesses, as the site of Marble Falls High School graduation in the 1930s, and as a dance hall named Casino Royale.

Around 1900, these unidentified individuals are seen fishing from the ledges at the falls. Women's clothing, including long skirts, long sleeves, and wide-brimmed hats, guarded against the hot Texas sun. They used fishing poles that were typical of fishing gear at the time. At right, the Marble Falls factory can be seen. (HB.)

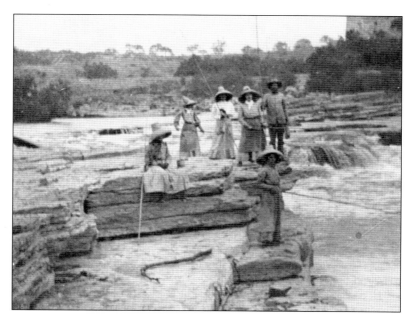

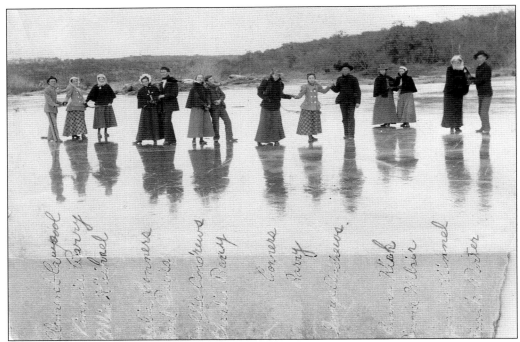

The falls froze solid on February 11, 1899, allowing this picture to be taken of a group wearing winter clothing and standing on the ice. It looks as if they were skating. Old-timers remembered, also, that rancher Bob Jay was able to ride his horse across the frozen lake that day.

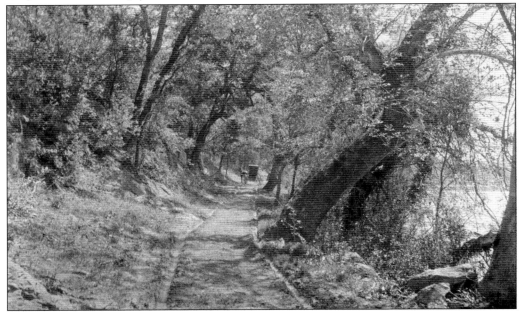

A beautiful tree-lined drive on the south side of the Colorado River, running west from the bridge, became known as Lover's Lane. Because that road often flooded, a new, safer road had to be built in the 1920s. Blasting of rock cliffs was necessary to create Farm to Market Road 2147, which runs westward toward Horseshoe Bay.

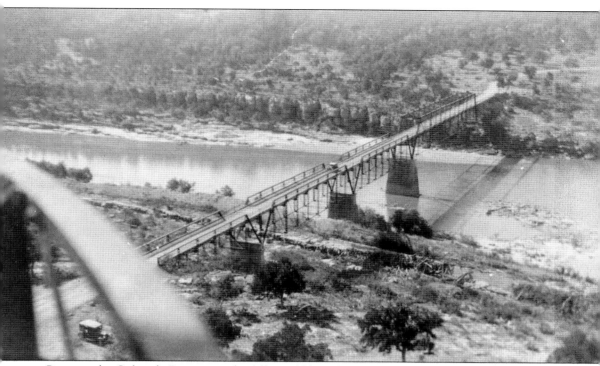

Crossing the Colorado River near the falls could be a difficult matter for travelers. In 1885, the Marble Falls Ferry Company was chartered by Johnson with W.H. and John Roper. When area residents began talking about building a bridge, Johnson and his partners conveyed Marble Falls town lots as bonding to the Gorton Bridge Company so that they would build the iron structure. The first Marble Falls bridge across the Colorado River was built in 1891 as a toll bridge. Citizens in the southern part of the county protested the toll and brought enough pressure on Burnet County officials that the group voted in 1896 to buy the bridge for $16,000 and allow free passage. (HB.)

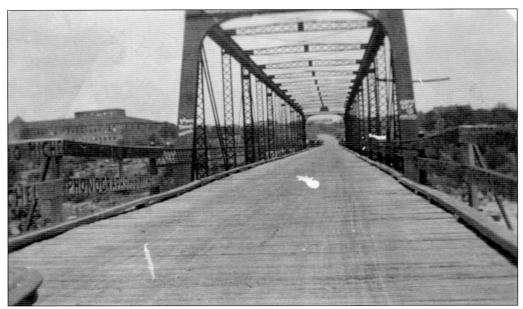

The 1891 bridge was built east of the factory. This view shows that, although it was mainly made of iron, its roadway and some side panels included lumber. Local merchants, especially Michel's Drug Store, painted advertisements on the side panels. This bridge was washed away in the Colorado River flood of 1935. (HB.)

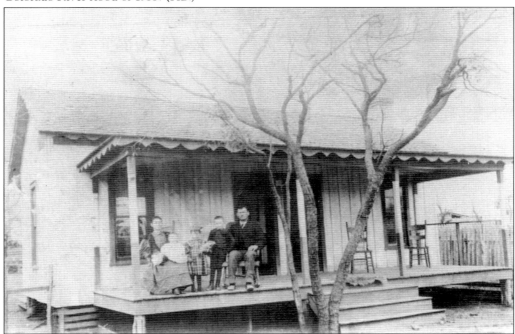

The John Milton Baird family is seen on their front porch in the 1890s. Baird worked for the Marble Falls Ferry Company, and his house was located on lots owned by the ferry company. The ferry was no longer needed after the first Marble Falls bridge was completed in 1891, and the Baird family later moved to Oklahoma. (FOCM.)

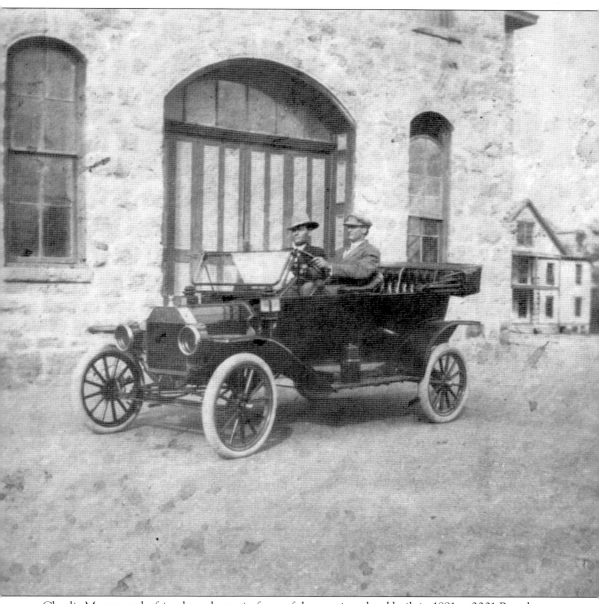

Charlie Mezger and a friend are shown in front of the granite school built in 1891 at 2001 Broadway, near Backbone Creek. The building was part of Adam R. Johnson's master plan for Marble Falls: the establishment of Alliance University. A wooden dormitory can also be seen. Although the university did not work out, the building continued to serve the students of Marble Falls in various other ways. It became the center of the school district formed in 1908, housing classes for all grades. After a new high school was built nearby in 1938, elementary classes remained in the old school. When a new elementary school was built in the 1950s, school administration offices occupied the old location until 2010. At that time, it became the permanent home of the Falls on the Colorado Museum. The Texas Historical Marker was added to mark the centennial of the structure. Charles Hundley was school superintendent at the time of that celebration. (Madolyn Frasier.)

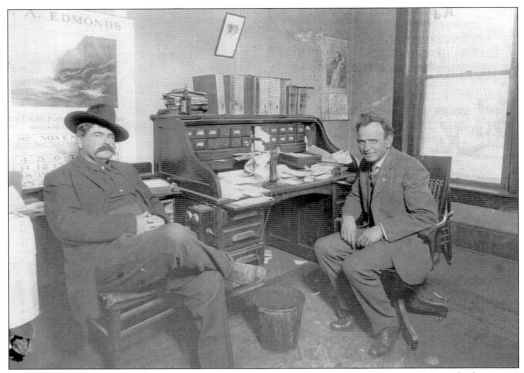

Attorney Guy Green is shown seated at his desk (right) in 1917 with an unidentified man in Waurika, Oklahoma. Green graduated in 1895 from Marble Falls Academy, the successor to Alliance University. After school in Marble Falls, he served as a sergeant during the Spanish-American War before becoming a lawyer. (Jean Eades.)

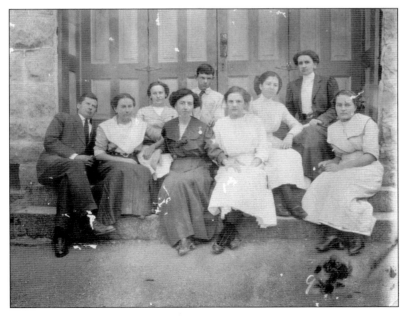

Students pose on the steps of the granite school building around 1900. Before the construction of this building and long before school attendance was required, children in Marble Falls were taught in various residences around town. In the 1880s, the Lacy family also built a school on their property north of Ranch Road 1431 and Arbor Lane. (FOCM.)

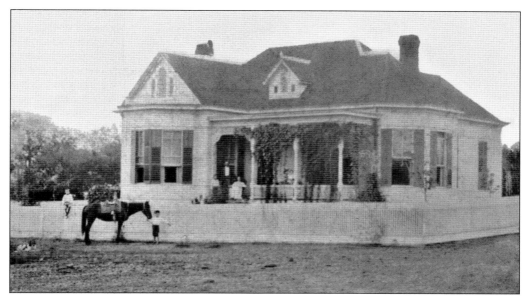

Juliet Johnson, daughter of the founder of Marble Falls, married George Christian in 1887. They built this Queen Anne–style house in 1892 and are pictured here on the front porch, surrounded by their children. Ivo B. and Mina Matern bought the house in 1908 and owned it for 51 years. Ivo, a merchant and rancher, also served as mayor of Marble Falls in 1937. (FOCM.)

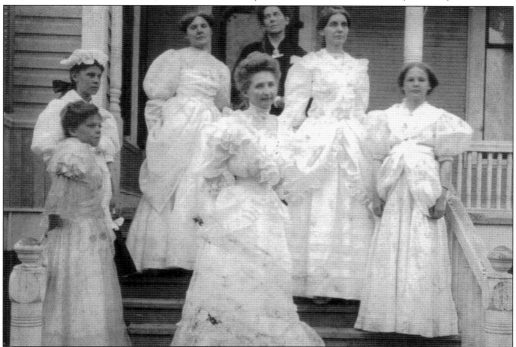

Juliet Christian posed with this group on the front steps of her home around 1900. The two in front are unidentified. Behind them stand, from left to right, unidentified, Ethel Johnson Guthrie (Juliet's sister), unidentified, Juliet Johnson Christian, and Josephine Christian. This home still is located at 603 Seventh Street in Marble Falls. (Texas Historical Marker) (FOCM.)

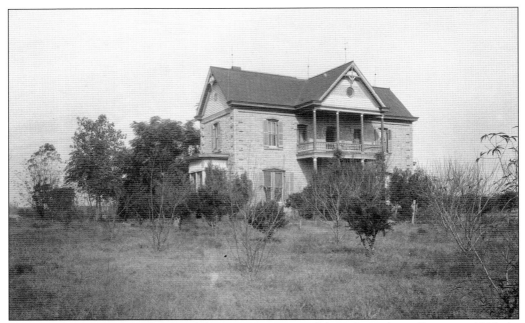

Brandt Badger (1839–1920), a Confederate veteran, moved from Gonzales to Burnet in 1885. As one of the founders of Marble Falls, he built this elegant "granite rubble" house in 1888. The structure has eight rooms and six fireplaces. Badger lived in the house until his death, and it was owned by the family until 1943. (Texas Historical Marker.)

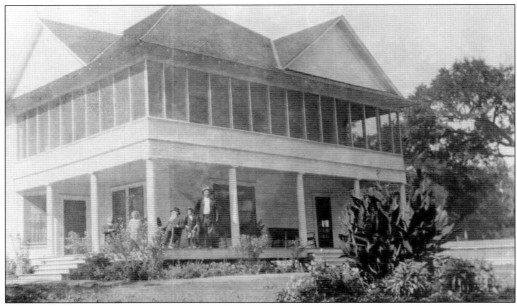

Darragh family members are pictured about 1912 on the front porch of their home at Granite Mountain. They are, from left to right, Clyde Lacy, Allie Mary Darragh, Thomas Darragh Sr., Steinmetz Darragh, and Thomas Darragh Jr. Thomas Darragh Sr. moved from Ireland to New York City, where he married Sarah Kinkaid. They brought their family to Marble Falls in the 1890s. (Mary Lucas.)

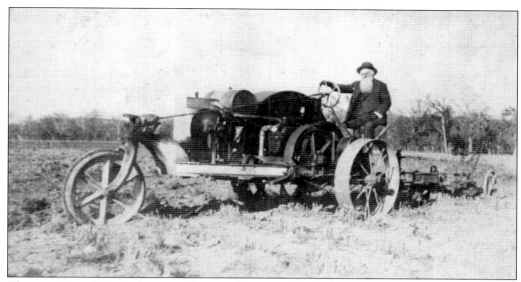

Thomas Darragh Sr. is shown working with a two-cylinder bull tractor in the field at Granite Mountain. He moved in the 1890s from New York to purchase the granite property, and his descendants continued to work and to live at the mountain until the 1950s, when they sold it to Cold Spring Granite of Minnesota. (Mary Lucas.)

Rosa Ellen Phelan married Thomas Darragh Jr. in Marble Falls in 1896. She had been a teacher before she married and later owned a business on Main Street, not far from Michel's Drug Store. She and others in the Phelan family were very supportive of the First Christian Church on Main Street. In the 1930s, she had a granite home built on Main Street. (Mary Lucas.)

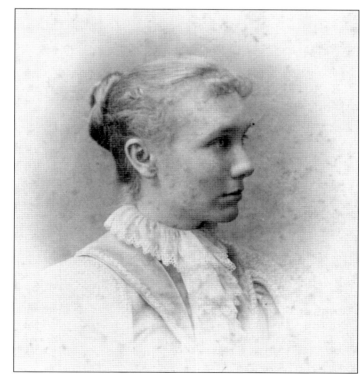

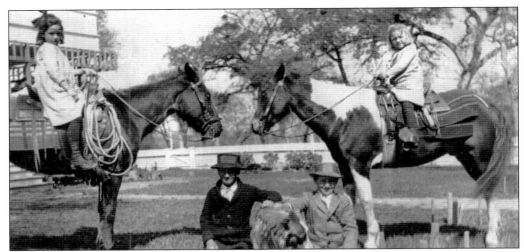

Children of Thomas Darragh Jr. and Rosa Darragh are shown playing near their Granite Mountain home. On the left, Attie Mary rides a horse named Dick, and to the right, Josephine rides Dan Patch. Between them are their brothers Steinmetz (left) and Herbert with their dog. (Mary Lucas.)

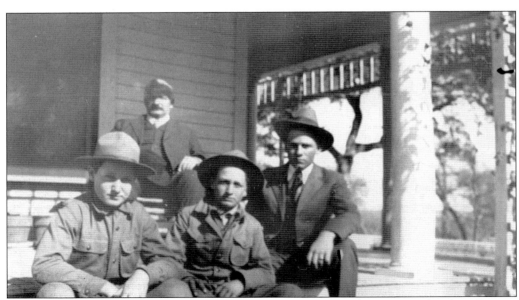

Wearing Boy Scout uniforms, Herbert (left) and Steinmetz Darragh are pictured at their Granite Mountain home about 1915. Their brother, Thomas E. Darragh, is shown at right. Seated behind them is their father, Thomas Darragh Jr. (Mary Lucas.)

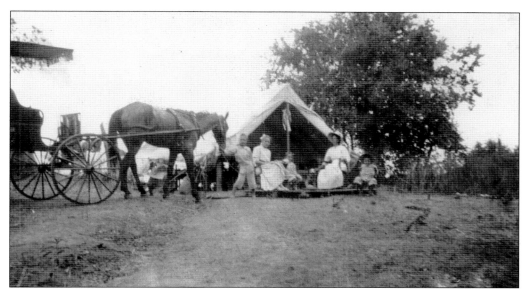

The Darragh family is shown camping on the Colorado River about 1910. Their Granite Mountain property stretched out along the river to include what the family called "the Shoals." The men used trotlines for fishing and did not need a boat. (Mary Lucas.)

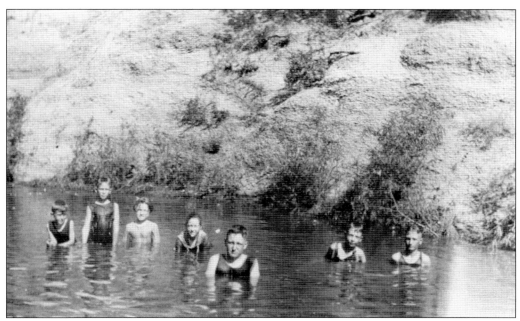

This swimming hole on Backbone Creek was a popular summer location for the Darraghs. The creek ran very near their Granite Mountain home. A cotton gin was located nearby. (Mary Lucas.)

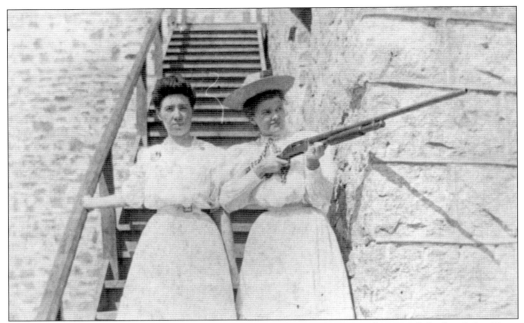

Marble Falls had telephone service in 1899, operated from the second story of the bank building at Main and Second Streets. Michel's Drug Store had the first telephone. Every call was handled by operators, such as the two posing here. Dial telephones came in 1955, replacing two separate telephone systems that had developed in the town. (FOCM.)

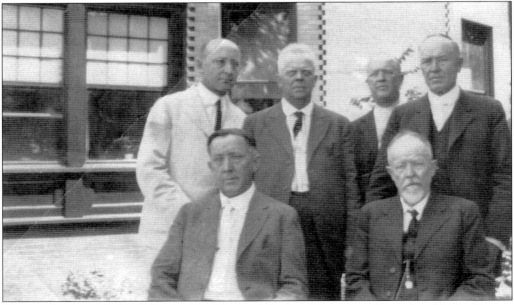

The first bank in Marble Falls, the First National Bank, still stands at Second and Main Streets. Other banks followed. Rudolph Ebeling (standing second from left) conducted business around 1900 under the name of the Ebeling Banking Company. The bank was located in today's Old Oak Square, and its vault remains at its original site. Also pictured in unknown order are G.L. Hundley, L.W. Hooper, C.M. Marrs, and Walter Giesecke.

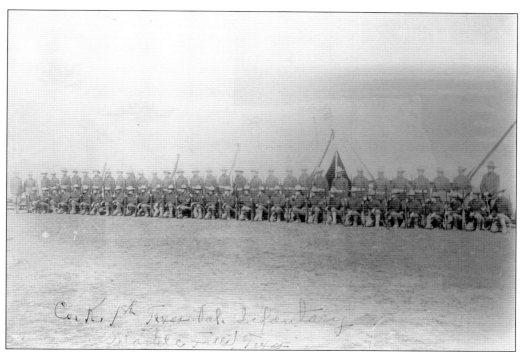

Co. K, 1st Texas Vol. Infantry Marble Falls Texas

Pictured are Marble Falls volunteers who made up Company K, 1st Texas Infantry, US Army, for service during the Spanish-American War in Cuba in 1898. H.E. (Pete) Faubion, V.M. Lacy, and two of Adam Johnson's sons, Robert and Adam Jr., were among those who trained in San Antonio for the Rough Riders.

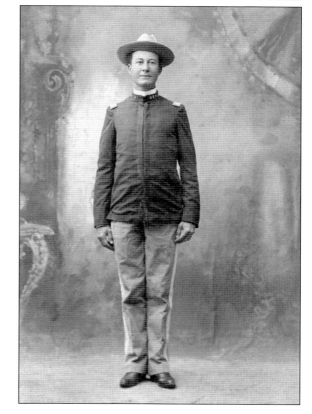

One of the volunteers in Company K was Lt. Ira Dawson of Marble Falls, shown here in his US Army uniform. After the war, he served as a physician in his hometown when the town voted in favor of incorporation in 1907. (FOCM.)

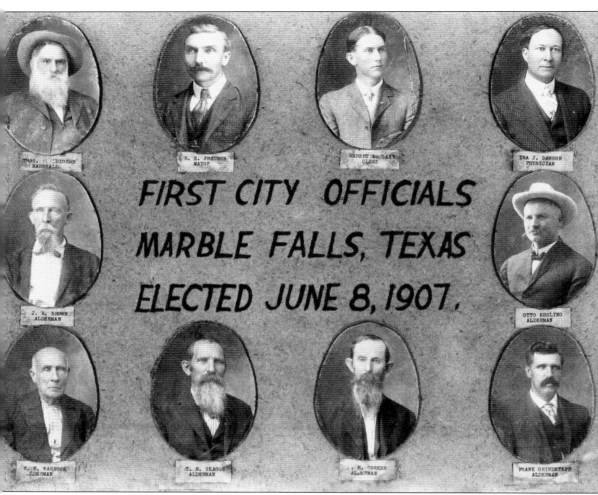

FIRST CITY OFFICIALS
MARBLE FALLS, TEXAS
ELECTED JUNE 8, 1907.

Marble Falls incorporated on May 18, 1907, in order to qualify for free state schooling and organize the Marble Falls Independent School District. The vote was 75 in favor and 67 opposed. Pete Faubion, owner and publisher of the *Marble Falls Messenger*, had supported incorporation. Electric lights were available in Marble Falls homes that year, and the newsman hoped the town would get cleaned up and that hogs would not run on the streets. Before the first election on June 8, 1907, city matters were handled by Adam R. Johnson and other town founders. Pictured in the top row, second from the left, is first mayor Robert E. Johnson. The son of Adam R. Johnson, he was born in Burnet in 1868. Elected aldermen were J.R. Brown, Otto Ebeling, W.H. Warnock, T.B. Skaggs, J.H. Corker, and Frank Grindstaff. Former infantryman Dawson was officially the city physician, Thomas F. Odiorne served as marshal, and Herbert Tate was the town clerk.

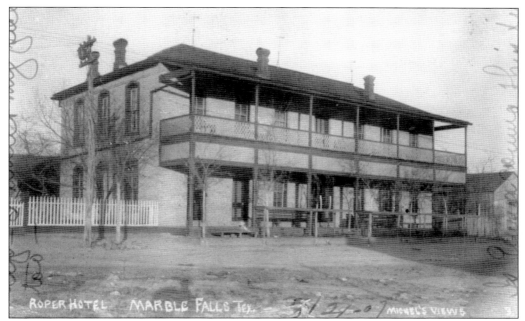

With the coming of the railroad, George and Elizabeth Roper built the Roper Hotel one block east of Main Street in 1888. As one of the earliest hotels in the area, the Roper became the stop for traveling salesmen, vacationing Texas politicians, and tourists. Salesmen were allowed to set up their displays at the hotel so that prospective customers could stop in.

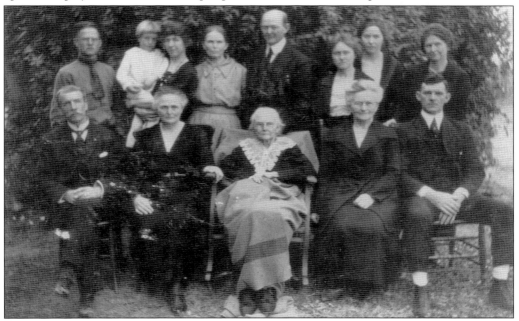

Roper family members are photographed at the family hotel in 1922. They are, from left to right, (first row) Louis Hester, Emma Roper Carleton, Elizabeth Hockenhull Roper, Lucinda Roper Robinson, and unidentified; (second row) Jack Roper, Robert Clark, Liska Roper Clark, Molly Banks, Arthur Roper, Marguerite Hester, Maud McDaniels, and Myrtle Gallagher. (HB.)

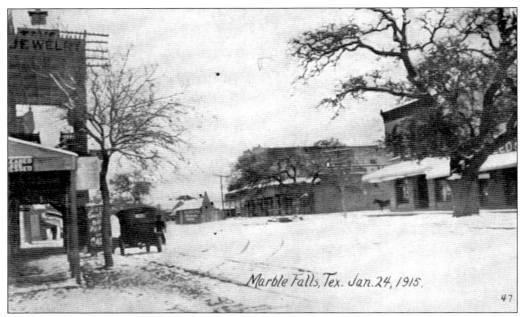

Marble Falls, Tex. Jan. 24, 1915.

47

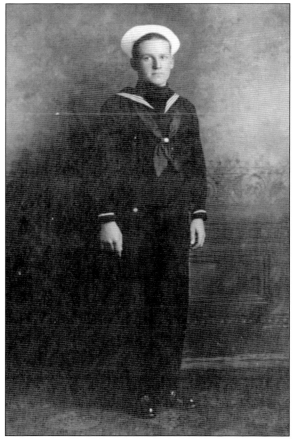

This postcard from January 24, 1915, shows Main Street in Marble Falls after a winter snow. In the view toward the north, several trees can be seen in their Main Street locations at that time. The three-story Michel building is at left. The central building, located at Third and Main Streets, has been used for a variety of businesses through the years and is the only pictured building that is still standing.

During World War I, Marble Falls men were among those who were called to serve their country. Thomas Elbert Darragh of Marble Falls had his picture taken at the family home while on leave from the US Navy. He died of an illness while stationed in Massachusetts and was buried in the Marble Falls Cemetery in 1918. (Mary Lucas.)

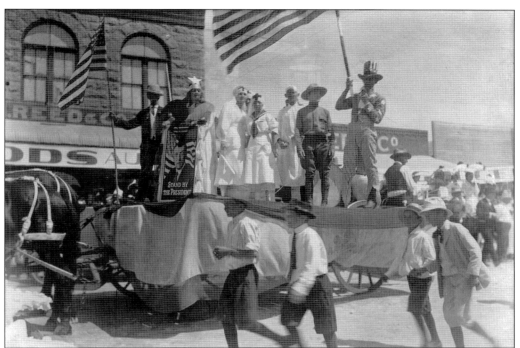

The Armistice Day horse-drawn parade entries along Main Street celebrated the end of World War I on November 11, 1919. This photograph shows a float with local residents dressed as Uncle Sam and as Army personnel. During the war, everyone had attended rallies at the opera house to buy war savings stamps. After the armistice was signed, the kaiser was hung in effigy from an oak tree in the middle of Main Street.

Adam R. Johnson (center) is pictured in 1918, during World War I, with two of his grandsons, sons of his daughter Juliet Johnson Christian. Walton J. Christian (left) and George E. Christian (right) stand with their grandfather outside the Johnson home in Burnet. After the war, Walton worked for the railroad commission, and George was a lawyer and a judge. (Jo Christian Babich.)

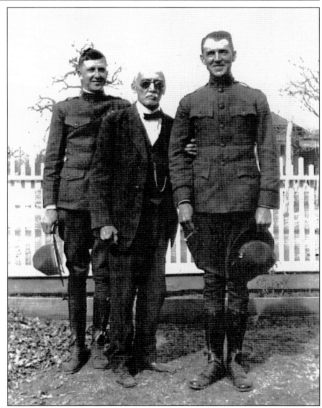

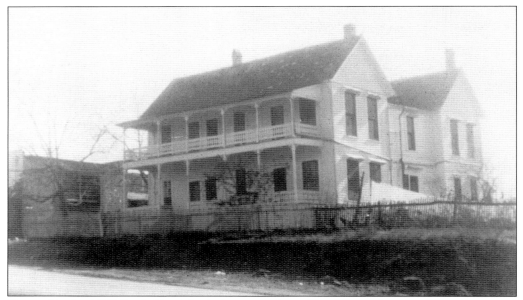

Pictured is the 1907 Bredt Hotel, built facing north on Third Street between Main Street and Avenue J. The hotel was soon sold to Gertrude Wallace. The two-story Wallace House enjoyed good times when tourism increased in the 1920s, even though many people preferred to camp for free along the river in the pecan and oak groves. (FOCM.)

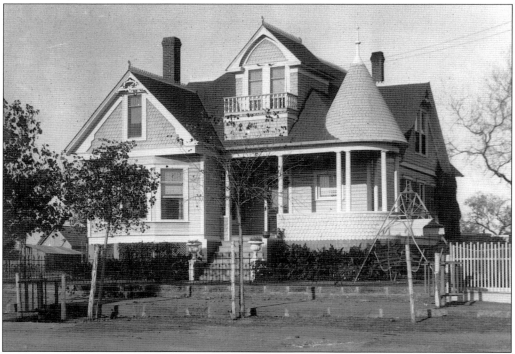

The R.T. Badger home that once stood on Avenue H is shown as a reminder of how important historical preservation practices can be. Whether the house was moved to make way for a new highway or a new business, the fact remains that its beauty is gone from the town.

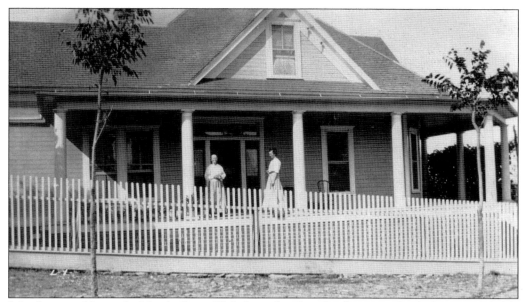

John Lacy and his wife, Maude Curry Hale Lacy, lived in this home on Sixth Street in Marble Falls. Pictured on the porch are Maude Lacy (left) and her sister-in-law Pearl, who married Emmett Carl (Charlie) Mezger.

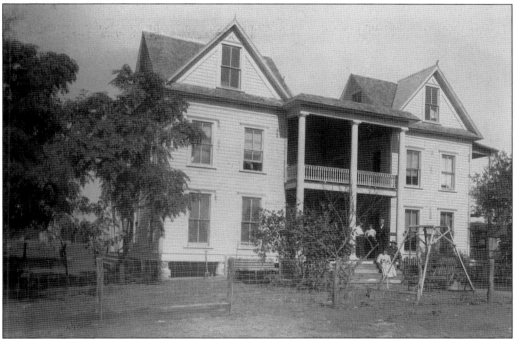

Adam R. Johnson built a Marble Falls home for family members in 1888. Pictured on the front steps are, from left to right, (first row, seated) "Miss Lou" Johnson and son Robert Eastland Johnson (first mayor of Marble Falls); (second row, standing) Roberta Williams, Julia Williams, and Johnson. Built at Second Street and Avenue G, the house faced south, with a view of the Colorado River and the falls.

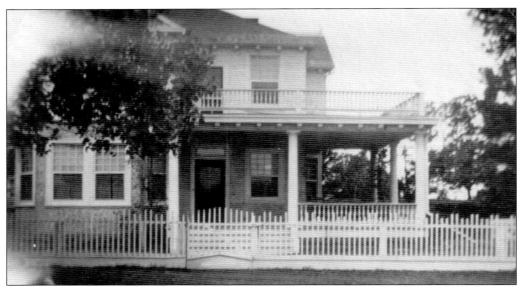

Pictured is the Rudolph Ebeling home that was located on US Highway 281 at Seventh Street. It was known as the Heinatz home, the name of the original owner. The home burned before 1950. (Deanna Bradshaw.)

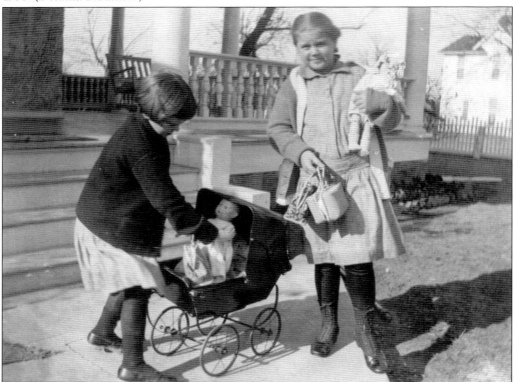

Helen Marie (left) and Hulda "Nookie" Ebeling, children of Rudolph and Hulda Ebeling, are shown playing at their home in Marble Falls. The girls wore dresses and dark stockings to play with their dolls and a doll buggy. (Deanna Bradshaw.)

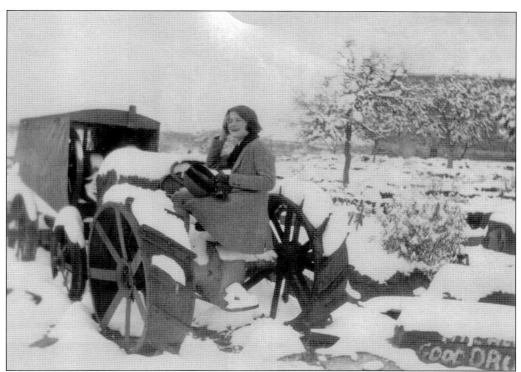

Frances Ebeling, oldest daughter of Hulda and Rudolph Ebeling, is pictured in a playful pose on a tractor after a snowfall in the Marble Falls area in the 1920s. After graduating from Marble Falls High School and completing college, Frances returned to teach for a short time in her hometown. (Deanna Bradshaw.)

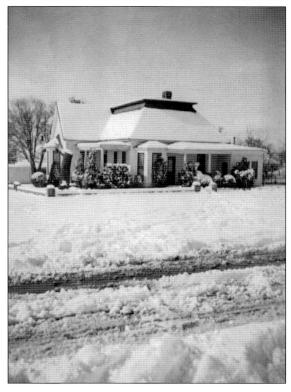

Another snow scene, this photograph shows the Sixth Street home of Robert and Ella Jay, parents of Lois Jay Darragh. The house remains in its original location in eastern Marble Falls, displaying fine woodwork typical of Victorian-style homes. Bob Jay Darragh spent happy times visiting his grandparents at the site. W.D. Yett had the two-story home with mansard roof built in 1898. (Ann Darragh.)

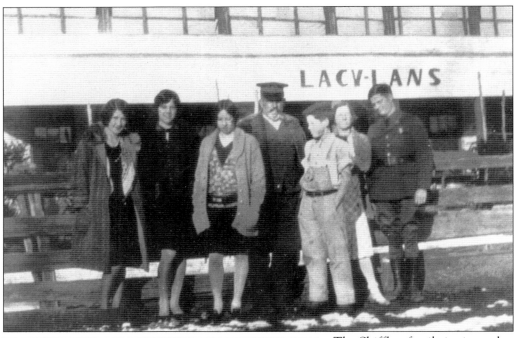

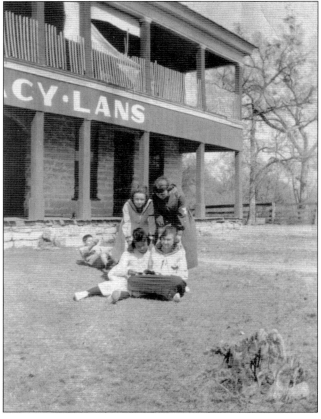

The Shifflett family is pictured in the 1920s at their ranch home, Lacy Lans, on the north side of Marble Falls. They are, from left to right, Nan, Frances, Mary, father George Hardin Shifflett (wearing his son's A&M College cap), Alfred, mother Nettie Lacy Shifflett, and Hardin Jr. (in his A&M College Corps uniform). The younger Hardin died of appendicitis soon after graduation. A&M College became Texas A&M University at College Station. (Linda Atkinson.)

Unidentified girls are pictured in front of the Lacy Lans home in the 1920s, when it belonged to Nettie Lacy—a descendant of Frank Lacy— and her husband, George H. Shifflett. The house was built in two parts with a dogtrot in between. The upstairs sleeping porch can be seen. In recent times, the structure has been remodeled to a one-story house. (Linda Atkinson.)

On June 14, 1935, the raging Colorado River, carrying extra water from the Llano River, began its damage of the 1891 Marble Falls bridge. Old-timers reported that the river rose at the rate of 10 feet per hour. Flooding was so heavy all across town that Backbone Creek kept children from getting home from the old granite school. (HB.)

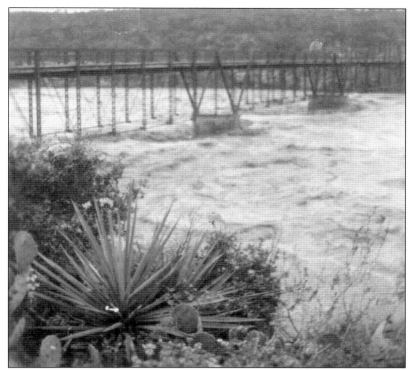

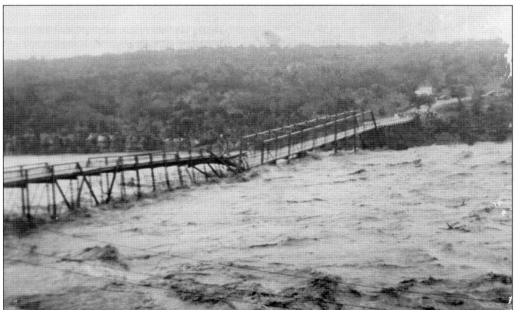

Photographs were taken from the north side of the Colorado in Marble Falls. People who watched the old bridge going down knew they had no way to prevent damage from heavy flooding. At the time, however, work was being done upriver on a series of dams that would soon bring protection. Buchanan Dam was well underway with over 1,000 employees, and work on the Inks Dam was getting started.

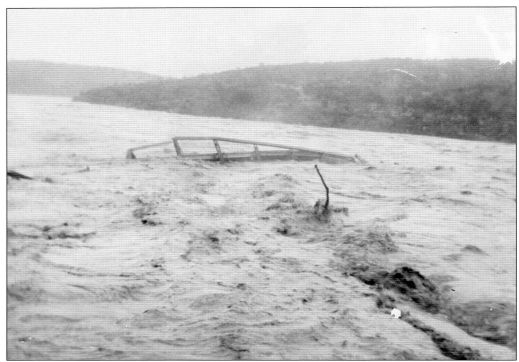

The Marble Falls bridge was gone—washed out—by 3:05 p.m. on June 14, 1935. At one time, the river rose to a height of 62 feet. It would take 15 years before six dams would be completed on the Colorado River in order to prevent the kind of damage that Marble Falls residents knew to expect from flooding.

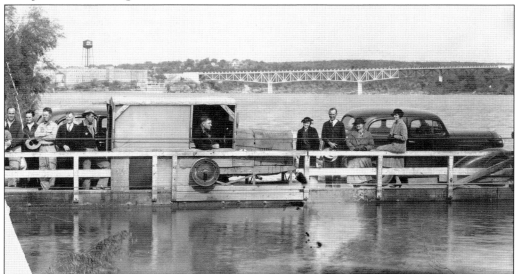

The state built a three-car ferry to operate until a new bridge could be built. Ferry service began again on the river on July 8, 1935. When the new two-lane, 936-foot-long bridge was dedicated in 1936, former mayor Birdie Harwood, on horseback, led the parade across the bridge into Marble Falls. It was the same year Marble Falls got its first fire truck.

Three

MAIN STREET

The first "main" street in Marble Falls was located near today's Avenue N, which runs from north to south and crosses the railroad, about two miles east of Granite Mountain. After the depot was built at the railroad, a few businesses and some homes were constructed nearby. The depot became an important gathering point for people, especially after postmaster John A. Roper moved the post office near the depot and passenger trains began to arrive.

Then, because that street was likely to be flooded when heavy rains fell on the headwaters of the Colorado and Llano Rivers, businessmen built on Avenue I, which was set on a higher ridge east and parallel to Avenue N. Before long, the avenue up on the ridge became known officially as Main Street. Even the town's jail was rebuilt near Main Street, where it remains, though it has never been used.

In 1890, businesses owned by the Farmer's Alliance began to benefit the growing township of Marble Falls. The alliance was credited with helping to build the university and the factory. Because the university was constructed on Broadway, which connected to North Main, students from throughout the settlement could easily reach it. The factory that sat on a large, flat area overlooking the falls seemed like a southern extension of Main Street.

Along with the growth of the new town came an increasing need for a bridge to facilitate crossing of the river. When an iron and wooden bridge was built across the Colorado in 1891, it connected with a street that led up to Main Street, thus helping to promote the building of more businesses and new homes along Main Street.

Progress was interrupted by fires on Main Street and by the great Colorado River flood of 1935, which washed the first bridge down the river. After the second Marble Falls bridge was completed in 1936 and the nation recovered from World War II, a new "main" street developed in Marble Falls as traffic increased across Burnet County. That roadway lies east of and parallel to Main Street and is known as US Highway 281.

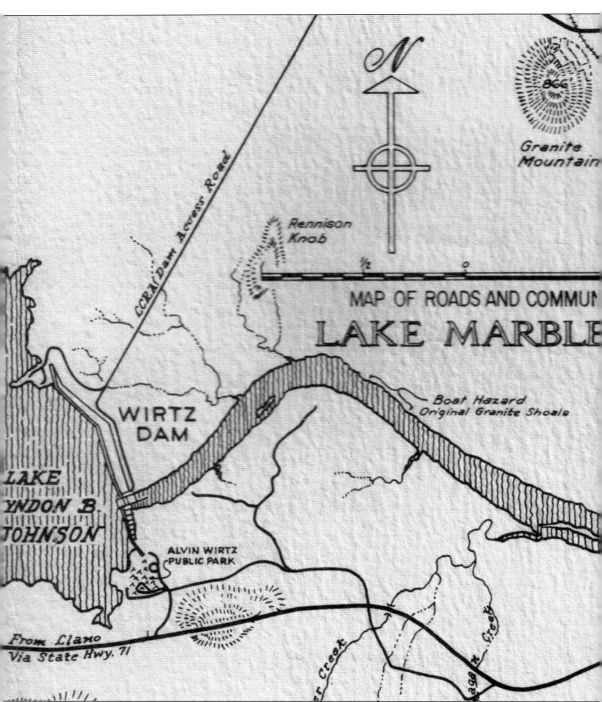

This map shows the area that benefited when the Lower Colorado River Association (LCRA) completed Max Starcke Dam south of the Marble Falls bridge in 1951. The Texas Legislature created LCRA in 1934 in order to tackle the flooding problems along the river above Austin. When the Marble Falls bridge washed away in a great flood in 1935, local people realized the importance of

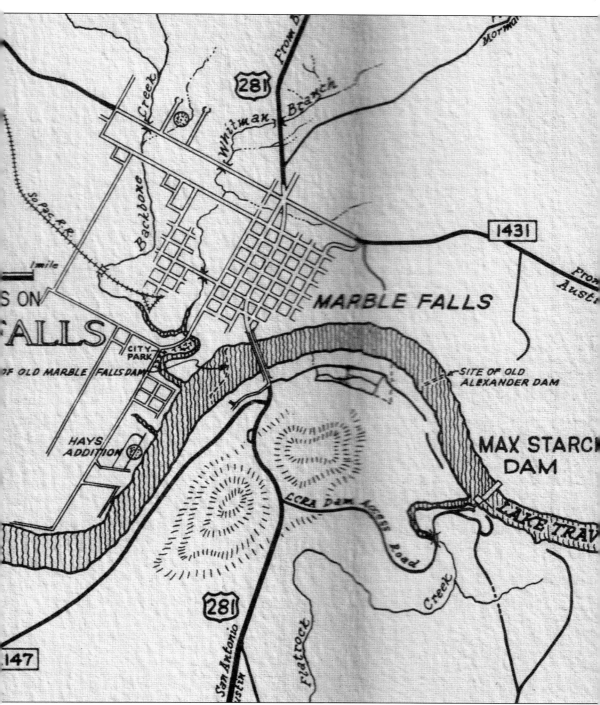

the work that LCRA had started upriver at Buchanan Dam. The "little dam" next to the factory and the Alexander dam east of the bridge were inundated during construction of the new dam. The Max Starcke Dam was the last of a stair-step chain of six dams above Austin. It took 19 months and $7 million to construct, and when completed, it created Lake Marble Falls, a constant-level lake.

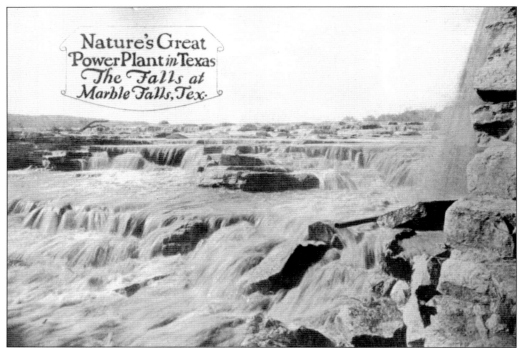

By 1910, Marble Falls community leaders contracted with a publicity company to create a booklet advertising the business opportunities in town. The booklet cover, pictured here, included the slogan, "Nature's Great Power Plant in Texas."

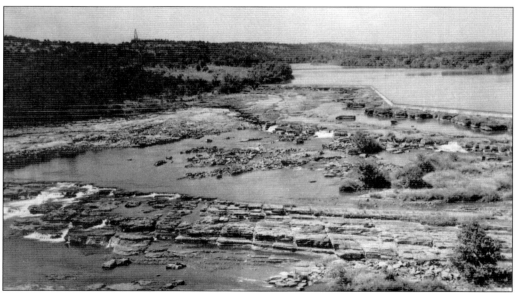

In the 1920s, when the town wanted more reliable power to provide water and electricity, a concrete dam, the "little dam," was built to direct river water to the powerhouse of the old factory building. The plant was used by the Lower Colorado River Authority to supply power and light in the construction of Hamilton (Buchanan) Dam in 1935.

Local trail driver Arthur Hays is pictured in Wichita, Kansas, around 1900. In the early days of Marble Falls, ranch hands drove herds of local cattle to join larger cattle drives on their way to western and northern markets or to a North Texas railroad. (Jean Eades.)

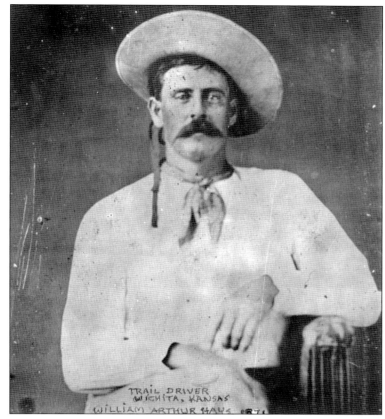

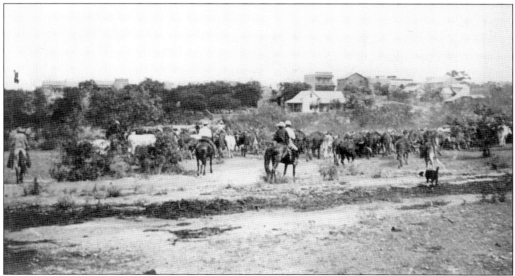

A rare photograph from the 1930s shows cattle that had crossed the Colorado into Marble Falls before they were driven around Main Street to the railroad stockyards. The white house at center was built by John Hickerson Burnam and his wife, Mabel Yett Burnam, when they moved to town from the ranch. (Jean Eades.)

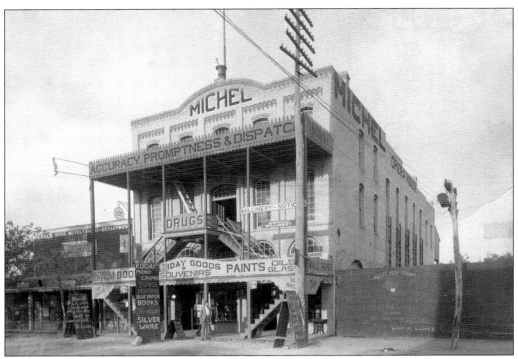

Ernst Gustav Michel lost a Main Street business to fire in 1905 and later built this three-story building. It had a drugstore on the first floor, an opera house to seat 300 on the second floor, and family living quarters on the third floor. Ollie Hundley played with a five-piece orchestra for opening-night festivities. The stage was used for early-day movies, road shows, high school programs, political rallies, and local fundraisers. (FOCM.)

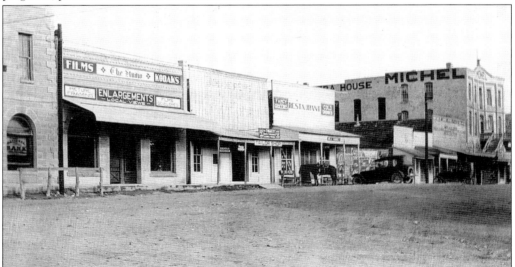

Main Street is shown as viewed from the south end of the street. In 1925, the dirigible *Hindenburg* hovered over the town and asked in a loud voice, "What town is this?" E.G. Michel got a megaphone and climbed up on the roof of his building to shout, "Marble Falls." After giving a "thank you," the historic ship continued on its way from Dallas to San Antonio.

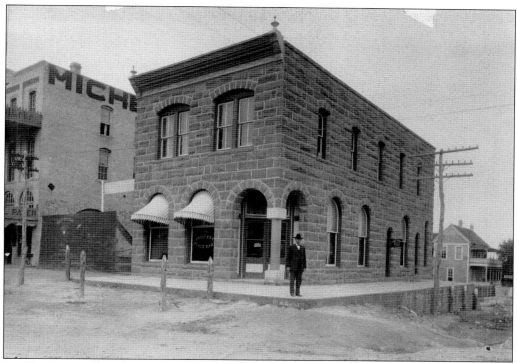

Dr. J.R. Yett stands in front of Citizen State Bank, the town's second bank, located on the north side of the opera house before the 1927 fire. His office was at the side of building. Bredt Hotel (later Gertrude Wallace's Hotel) can be seen behind and west of the bank. The cement sidewalk was laid in 1919. A theater built by R.O. Smith in the 1940s replaced the Citizen State Bank building.

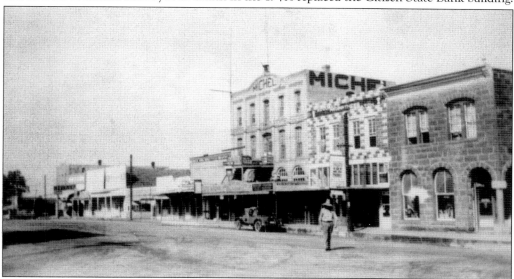

It was reported that burglars in McCoy Variety Store started a fire that destroyed seven buildings—including Michel's Opera House on the west side of Main Street—on April 15, 1927. However, the granite Home State Bank survived at Main and Second Street, and Michel's was back in operation in a one-story building by August. (FOCM.)

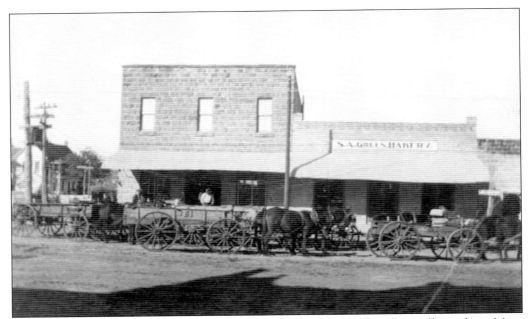

Green Bakery is shown on the north side of a two-story rock building that still stands on Main Street. Wallace House can be seen on the left. In 1924, the mayor and council of Marble Falls had the oaks on Main Street cut down, and the county road through town was graveled. In 1946, streetlights were installed in some places and roads were being paved.

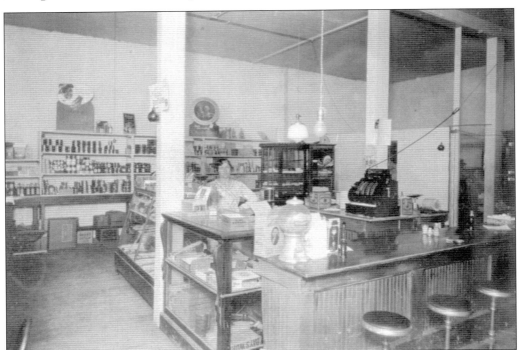

Mrs. S.A. Green is seen in the Green Bakery on the west side of Main Street. The business was north of a two-story rock building that still stands on Main at Third Street. (FOCM.)

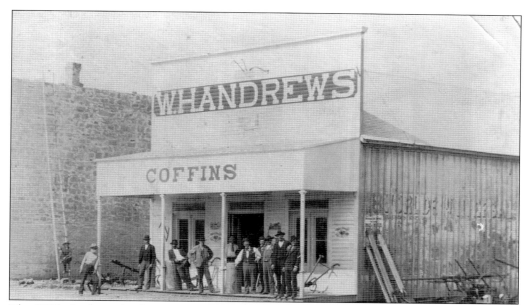

The W.H. Andrews implement company advertised the fact that they had coffins for sale. At other times, coffins were available at other Main Street sites, or people often crafted their own. Whatever the source of the coffins, customers usually made their own fabric linings for them.

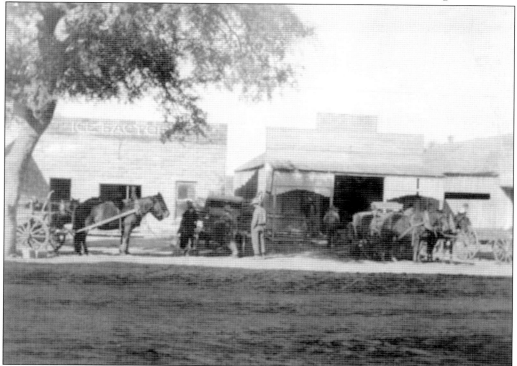

Tom and Ed Odiorne built an ice factory that opened in Marble Falls in 1910. Customers could buy 300 pounds of ice for $1 or could have 25 pounds delivered to a home for 15¢. In 1929, Texas Power & Light took over the town's electricity and the ice plant.

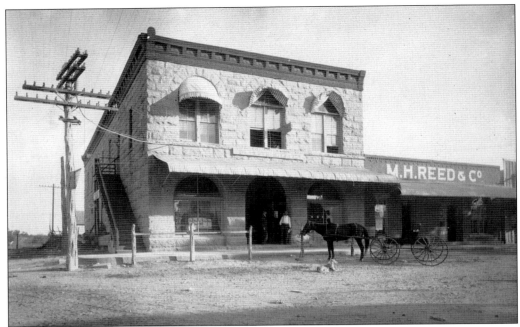

M.H. Reed & Company was a department store located on the southeast corner of Third Street at Main in the early 1900s. Later known as the Cholett store building, it was torn down mid-century to make space for convenient parking between Main Street and today's city hall on Third Street at US Highway 281.

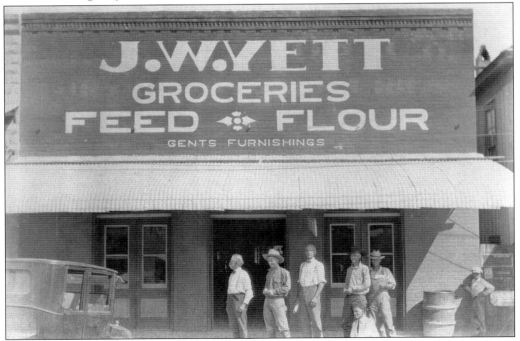

Porter Askew is pictured at the center of a group gathered in front of the J.W. Yett Grocery Store. Feed for farm animals and flour for household use, as well as "gents' furnishings," were available.

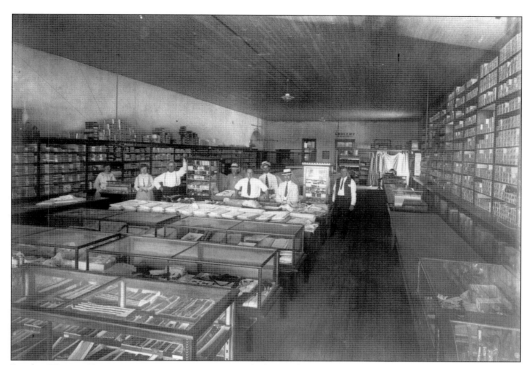

In the Turner-Evans store on Main Street, clerks and customers are pictured with a variety of goods that were available for purchase. A dressing room is evident, as is a sign directing customers to another area where groceries were sold.

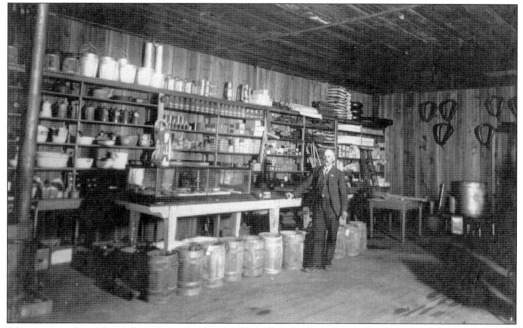

The owner of another Main Street store stands ready to sell products that answer the basic needs of rural area residents. Practical items available included horse collars, kegs of nails, and lanterns.

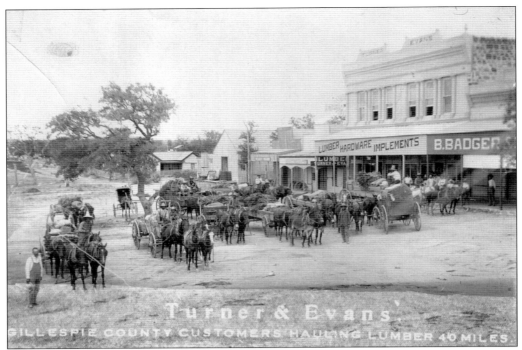

Turner & Evans Lumber and Hardware Store took over the Badger-McDonald store, located on Third Street at Main, about 1910. The stores served as background for this picture, captioned "Gillespie County customers hauling lumber 40 miles."

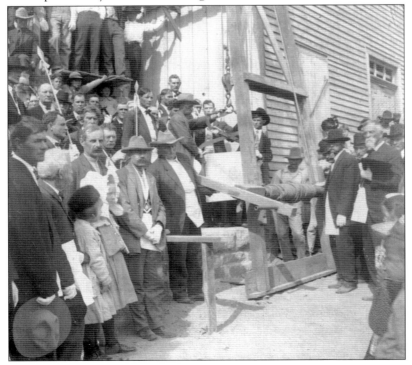

The cornerstone for Blazing Star Masonic Lodge on US Highway 281 at Third Street was set in November 1909. The new building replaced a two-story wooden lodge that was set on Main Street about 1888. At various times, the lower floor housed the *Marble Falls Messenger*, the Lois Anderson Memorial Library, and a small museum.

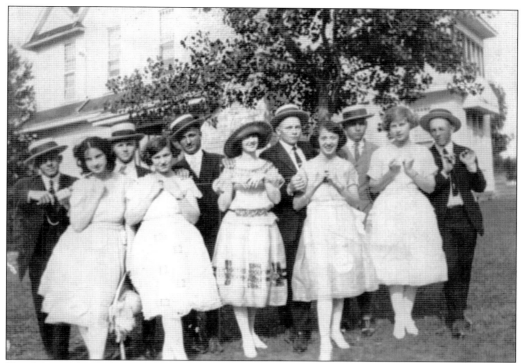

Hazel Brown (center) and her Marble Falls friends are shown dressed in flapper styles to go dancing in the 1920s. Hazel was the daughter of Ed G. Brown, a Marble Falls barber, and Sarah Hampton Brown from Fairland. After Hazel married R.O. Smith, they ran the Frances Hotel, which had belonged to R.O.'s father, Willis S. Smith. (Vashti Tucker.)

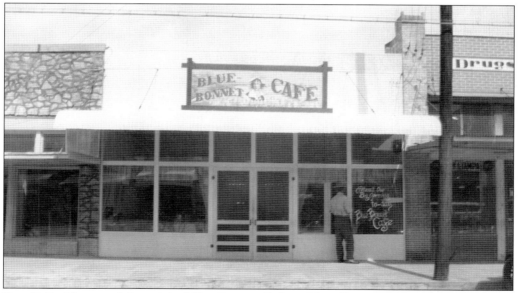

Otto E. Smith opened the original Blue Bonnet Café on Main Street in 1929. The Blue Bonnet was located next to the Michel's Drug Store that was built after the 1927 fire. The café remained there until Albert Haynes moved it to present-day US Highway 281 in 1946. (John Kemper.)

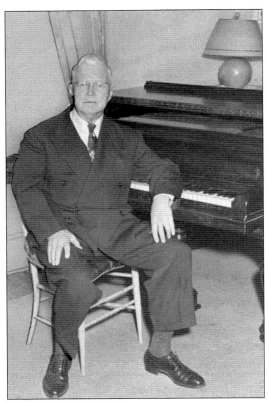

Well-known music composer Oscar J. Fox was a native of the Marble Falls area and a grandson of Rev. Adolph and Luise Fuchs, whose family settled the present Horseshoe Bay area. Oscar studied and lived in Europe and New York and was a favorite composer of Franklin D. Roosevelt. He gained fame with his collection of Western tunes such as "Home on the Range" and "Get Along, Little Dogies." (HB.)

The family of Oscar J. Fox set this granite memorial on the west side of US Highway 281 overlooking Marble Falls on May 27, 1962. His well-known song, "The Hills of Home," was inspired by the view of Marble Falls from high ridges south of the Colorado River. In 2012, the city moved the marker to a nearby location.

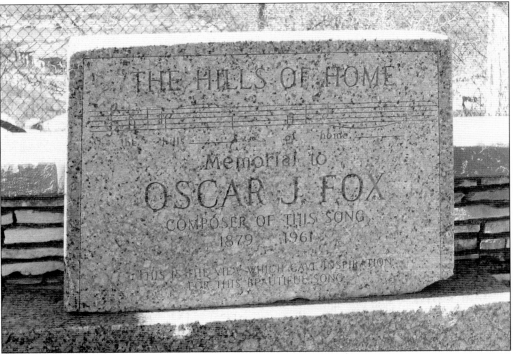

This copy of Oscar J. Fox's sheet music for his song "The Hills of Home" is displayed in the Falls on the Colorado Museum. The museum also has a copy of the memorial program that marked Fox's death on May 27, 1962.

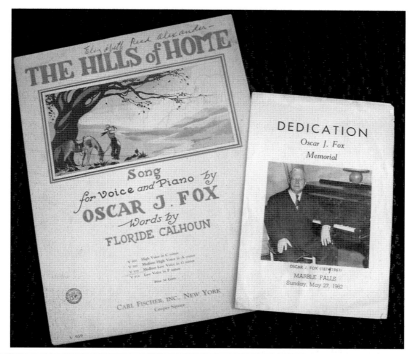

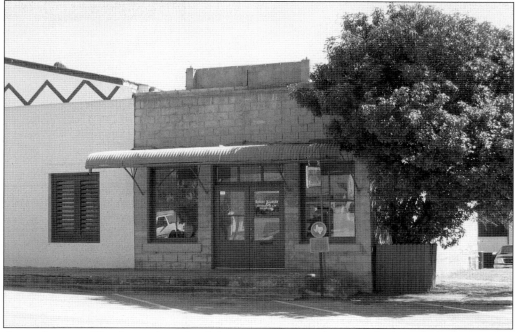

An early post office located south of the river was moved nearer the Marble Falls depot in 1886. Then postmaster William P. Cochran built this office in 1910, and mail service continued here until about 1950. The building was constructed of poured concrete and featured a central double door with three-pane transom, a simply detailed cornice, and stone parapet. (Texas Historical Marker.)

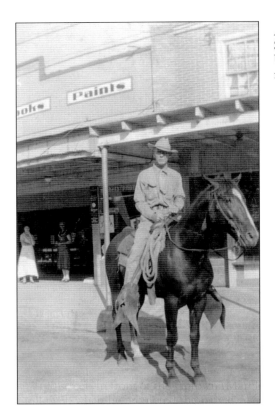

Arthur Ussery appeared on horseback on Main Street, in front of Michel's store, in the 1930s. Ussery was riding his horse Domino V, a stud reputed to have "good cow sense." (FOCM.)

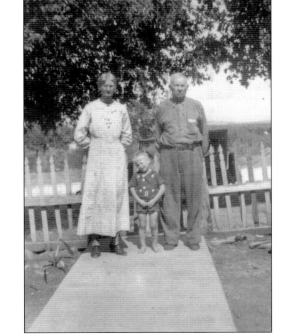

Grandparents Sam H. and Mattie Ussery are pictured in 1936 with grandson Lee at the Ussery home on Fourth Street. Lee was born in the front bedroom of the home. His parents were Gene and Anna Belle Bridges Ussery. Sam Ussery ran the first barbershop in Marble Falls. (Lee Ussery.)

Bob Jay is pictured on his horse at Jay's Stable, located near First Street at Main, around 1910. His brother Frank Jay owned a cedar yard south of the Colorado at the present location of the Holiday Inn Express.

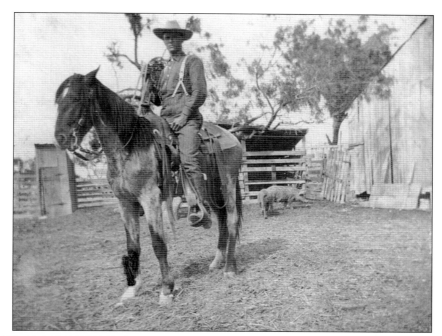

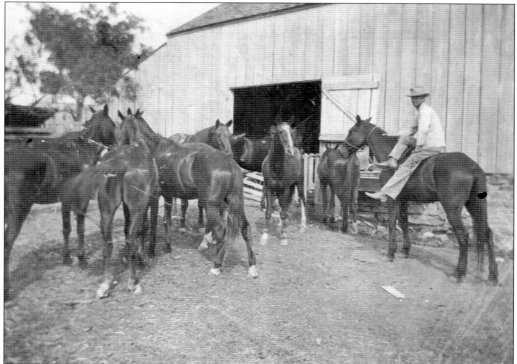

This is another view of horses at Jay's Stable on Main Street in times when horses were necessary for travel and for agricultural work. Someone from the stable usually met incoming trains to transport goods to Main Street or to provide transportation for train passengers, including salesmen, to local hotels.

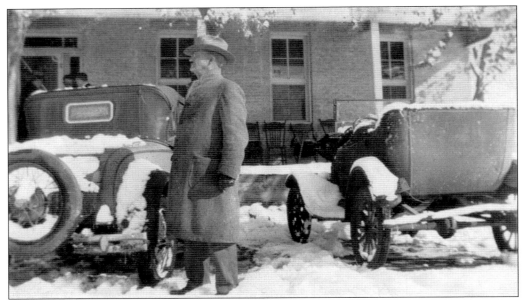

W.F. Smith, owner of the Frances Hotel (originally known as the Roper Hotel), is pictured in front of his hotel after a rare snowstorm in 1930. Smith was the Mobil Oil products distributor, with his business located north of the hotel, at the intersection of present day Highway 281 and Ranch Road 1431. (Vashti Tucker.)

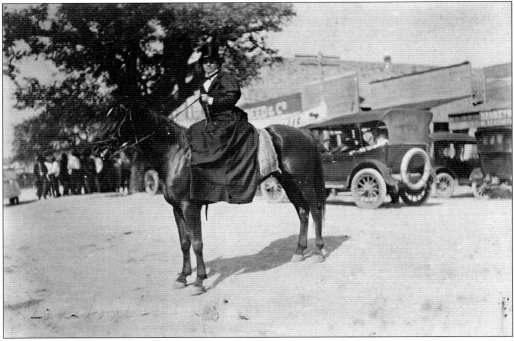

Ophelia "Birdie" Crosby Harwood was elected mayor of Marble Falls in 1917—before women gained the right to vote on March 28, 1918. The men of the town elected her to make needed changes in the community. She rode sidesaddle and wore a traditional black costume in many Marble Falls and San Antonio parades. Her platform called for a bigger and cleaner Marble Falls. (MF.)

Lillian Hooper of Marble Falls, the 1923 Burnet County Fair Queen, is shown in her parade costume. The queen reigned on the "minnow" float with two duchesses, Bess Francis and Margaret Lee Jones.

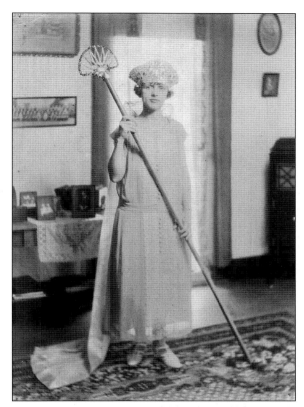

These youngsters, pictured riding a float on Main Street in the 1920s, honor men who served the United States during World War I.

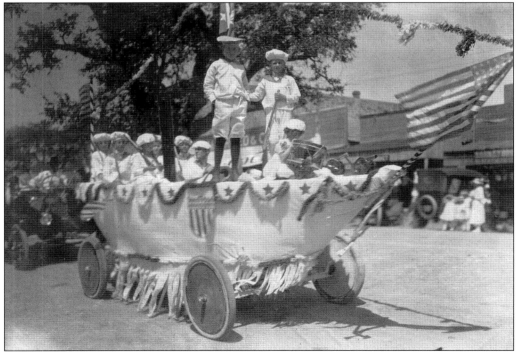

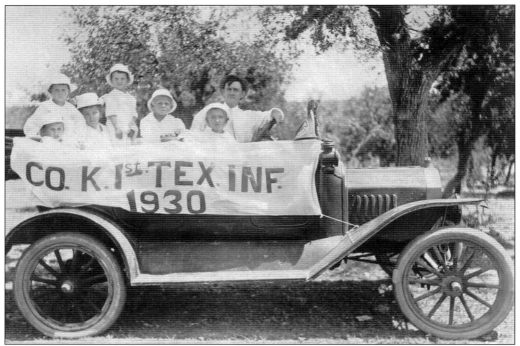

John Faubion, editor of the *Marble Falls Messenger,* drove this 1930 parade entry as a tribute to the men of Company K from Marble Falls, 1st Texas Infantry, US Army. The men served during the Spanish-American War in Cuba. Among those in the vehicle were Hodge McCleary, Carl Marrs, John Faubion Jr., and Richard Giesecke.

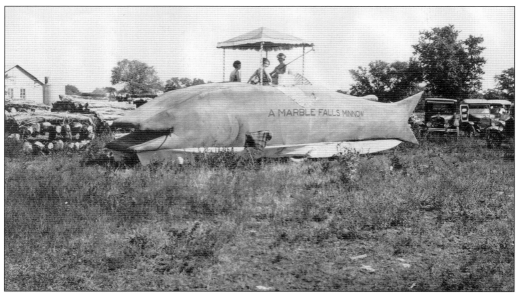

Lillian Hooper, 1923 Burnet County Fair Queen, is shown riding in a parade vehicle in the shape of a 32-foot-long yellow catfish labeled, "A Marble Falls Minnow." The "minnow" won best float in the Burnet County Fair and Rodeo Parade, which was then held in Bertram in July.

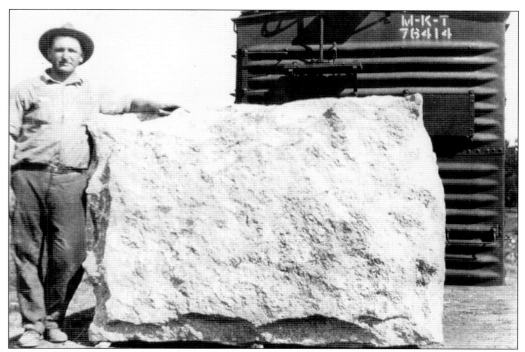

Herbert Darragh is pictured with granite that was on its way to New York City. The rock was to be used for a sculpture of a large granite ball supporting an eagle to be placed at Grand Central Terminal in New York City. The seawall in Galveston was built of local Texas Pink granite, as was the Burnet County Courthouse. (Mary Lucas.)

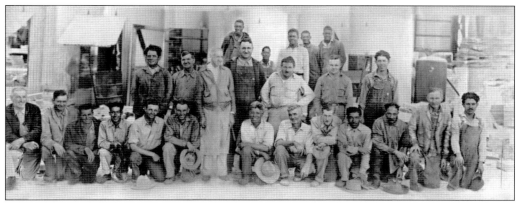

In 1930, Granite Mountain employees posed for this photograph. They are, from left to right, (first row) Charlie Fraser, Morris Crownover, Pee Wee Thurman, Juan Rodriguez, Clyde Lacy, N.A. Mason, A. Blanco, two unidentified, Martin Rodriguez, Francisco A. Perales, Grover Phinney, and Cosemedo "Shorty" Castanada; (second row) Carlos Blanco, unidentified, foreman Hoffman, Herbert Darragh, George Fraser, unidentified, and Pete ?; (third row) Tom Yett, Marion Yett, Joe Yett, Abe Lincoln, and Eugene Yett. (Mary Lucas.)

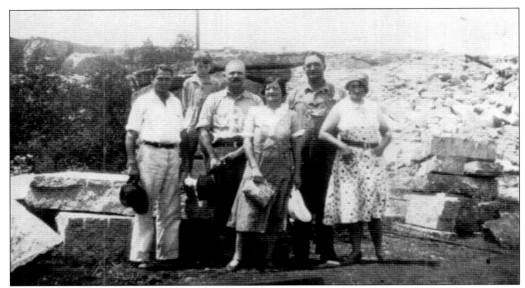

Darragh family members pose with members of the Falcone family. Mike Falcone was a partner in Darragh's business at one time. Pictured are, from left to right, George Darragh Jr., an unidentified Falcone grandson, Mike Falcone, Mrs. Falcone, Herbert Darragh, and an unidentified Falcone daughter-in-law. (Mary Lucas.)

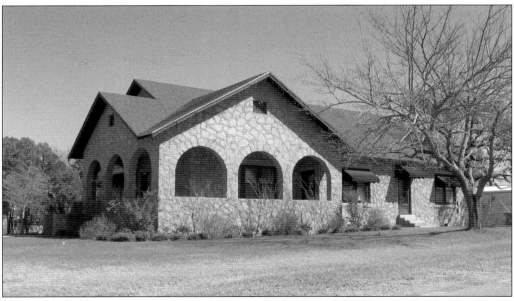

The Darragh granite home on Main Street was built after 1935, following the death of Rosa's husband, George Darragh Jr. The family wanted Rosa to have the house so that she would not have to make the drive from the mountain every day to work at her store. The Baptist church was located across the street, and the Alexanders and the Yetts lived nearby.

Rosa Phelan Darragh is pictured on Mother's Day at her Main Street home. Family gatherings were held at this house until her death in 1963. While the dams were being built on the Colorado, she sometimes moved into the basement of the house and rented out apartments or rooms to the workers. (Mary Lucas.)

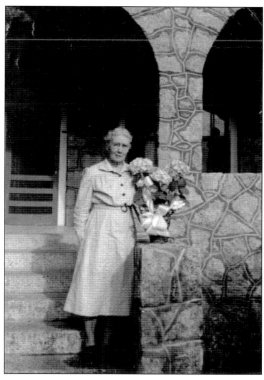

After the events at Pearl Harbor on December 7, 1941, citizens of Marble Falls were immediately involved in efforts on the home front to support their servicemen. Gasoline, tires, sugar, meat, and other items were rationed until the end of the war. This list of World War II servicemen was kept updated on Main Street. (Beulah Holland.)

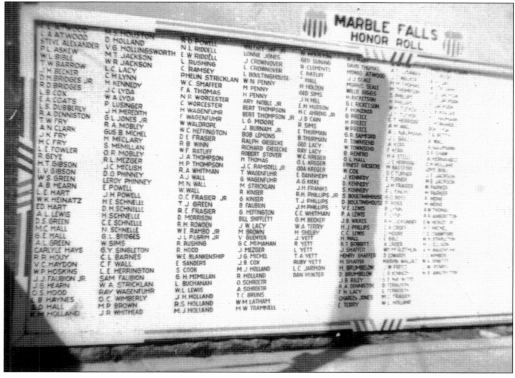

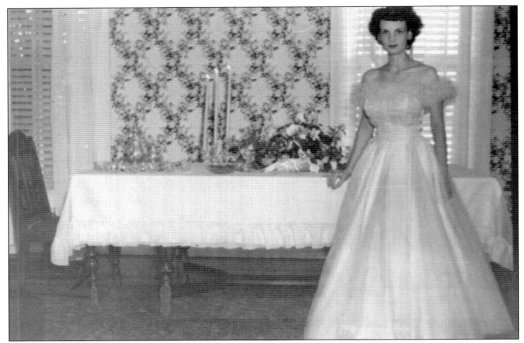

Vashti Smith is shown at a party to announce her engagement in August 1949. She was to marry Dale Tucker of Burnet. Vashti's parents, R.O. and Hazel Smith, and grandparents Willis S. and Mary Smith owned the Frances Hotel (originally named the Roper Hotel). The party was held in a large area that served as the hotel's living and dining room. (Vashti Tucker.)

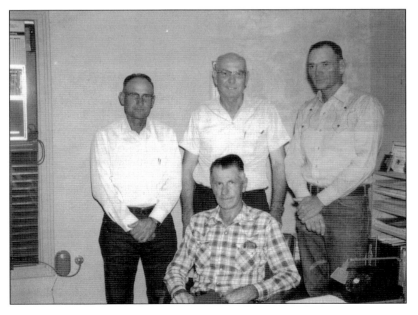

The Agriculture Service Club was important in Burnet County in the 1940s. President Landis Wier is seated in this photograph, and behind him stand, from left to right, treasurer R.E. Herbort, reporter Norman LaForge, and vice president Rudolph Holland. (Beulah Holland.)

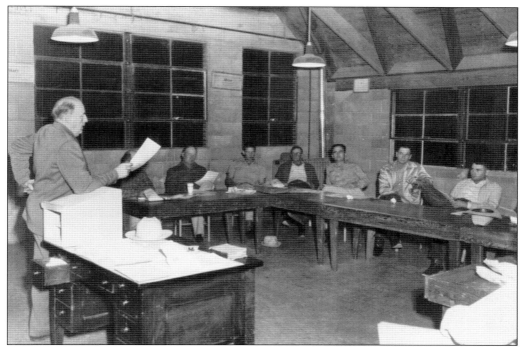

These World War II veterans are attending a class of the state veterans' agriculture school program. While some veterans chose to attend formal college classes, others attended classes like this one in order to improve their farming and ranching skills. (Beulah Holland.)

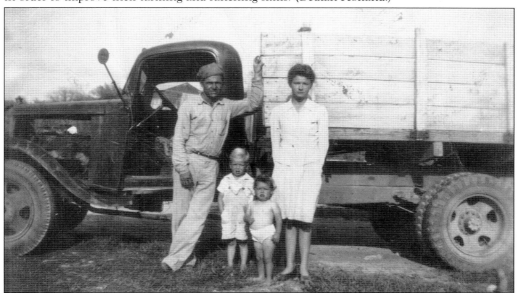

Earl Townsend and family are pictured with his cedar truck in Marble Falls in the 1940s. Also shown are his wife, Leona Jewel Bobbitt Townsend, and their children Ann and Earl Taylor Townsend. After Earl died young, his wife supported the family by providing cleaning services in the guesthouses at Granite Mountain. Earl and his brother Willie Townsend, a World War II casualty, were buried on the same day in 1948 in the Marble Falls Cemetery. (Ann Darragh.)

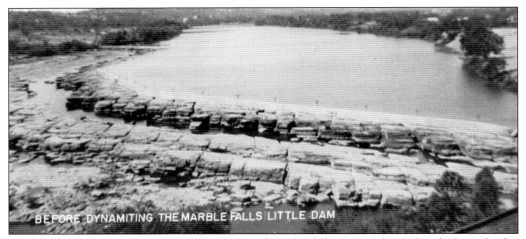

BEFORE DYNAMITING THE MARBLE FALLS LITTLE DAM

The "little dam" was a retainer wall constructed on the falls west of the Colorado River bridge in the 1920s. It directed river water toward the powerhouse of the factory in order to provide a more reliable source for electricity and water. The dam remained until 1952.

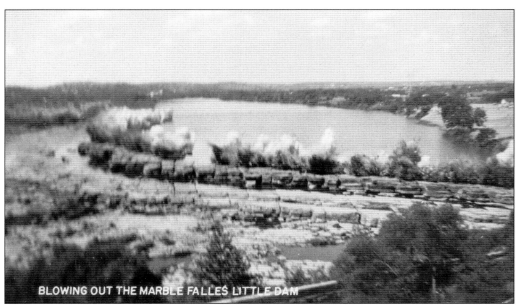

BLOWING OUT THE MARBLE FALLES LITTLE DAM

After the Alvin Wirtz Dam had been completed upriver from Marble Falls in 1951 and the Max Starcke Dam had been set in place, the little dam no longer had a purpose. This image shows the little dam as it was blown up to allow the waters of Lake Marble Falls to cover the area.

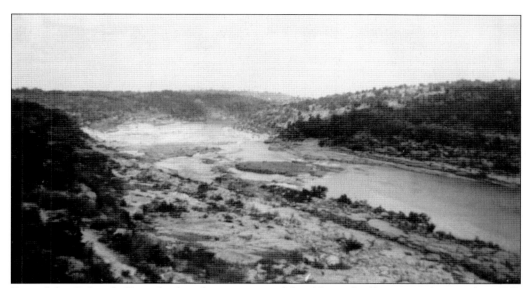

East of the Colorado River bridge, the remnants of the Alexander Dam were destroyed in 1951 to clear the way for Lake Mable Falls to move downriver to the Max Starcke Dam. Because the need for a dam was obvious, the Alexander Dam was begun east of the Marble Falls bridge in 1908; however, it was damaged by floods before it could be completed. (FOCM.)

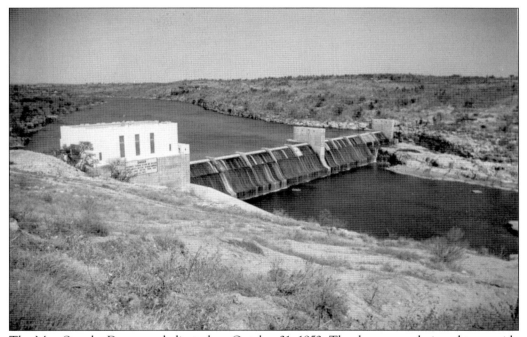

The Max Starcke Dam was dedicated on October 31, 1952. The dams were designed to provide hydroelectricity and flood control. Additionally, they also created waterways that turned the Marble Falls area into a resort destination.

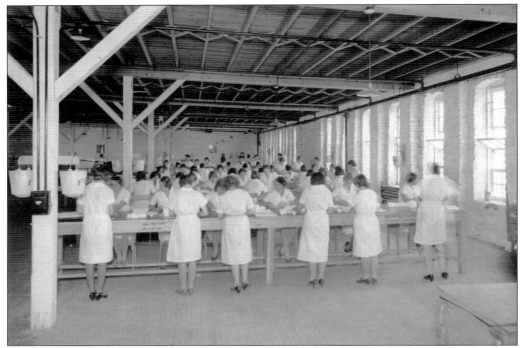

Employees of Certified Laboratories Inc. are pictured at work in the Marble Falls factory building in 1931. The Dallas-based firm produced surgical gauze and absorbent cotton for hospitals. The projected daily production was 100,000 yards of gauze and 2,500 pounds of cotton. (FOCM.)

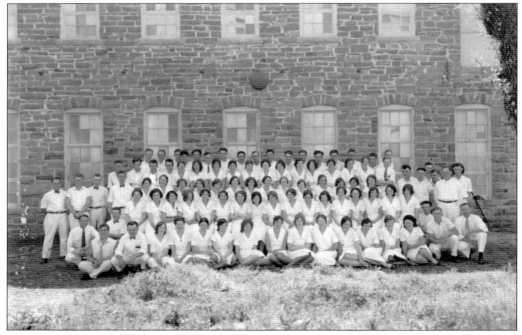

Employees of Certified Laboratories Inc. gather for a photograph outside the Marble Falls factory. In spite of high expectations, the company suddenly closed down after only one year. (FOCM.)

The factory was quiet during World War II. But in 1954, the Mathes Company purchased the old building to manufacture Curtis-Mathes air-conditioning units and metal boxes for the units. The company brought jobs to Marble Falls during the drought of the 1950s, when people really needed work. As shown in the picture, they were happy with seven years of steady paychecks. (Vashti Tucker.)

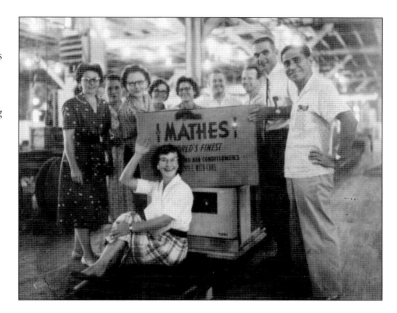

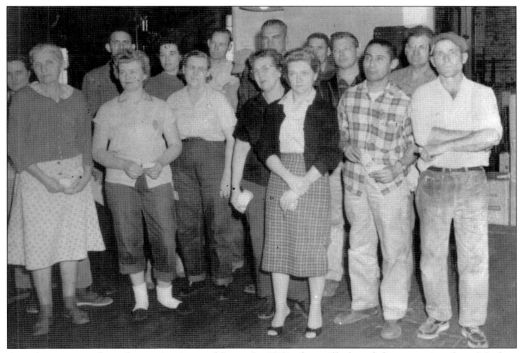

Another group of employees is pictured here. In 1961, the mill closed down again when Mathes sold the old building for $11 million. The factory was thought to be indestructible, but at 10:00 p.m. on August 8, 1964, it burned from unknown causes. The fire lasted two days, leaving charred rubble that was later pushed over into Lake Marble Falls. In 1998, a Hampton Inn and restaurants were built on the old factory site. (Jean Eades.)

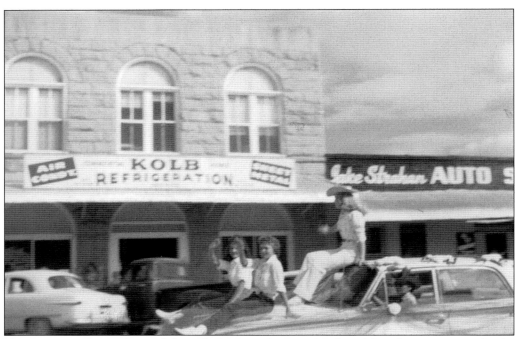

Names on storefronts changed through the years, but parades along Main Street continued to be important. Pictured here is part of a Rodeo Parade in the 1960s. (Beulah Holland.)

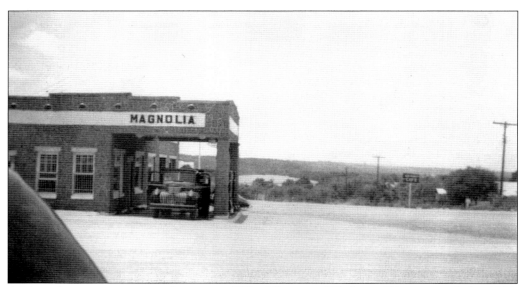

A Magnolia service station at the corner of Third Street and Highway 281 is pictured after 1946. At right, a sign directs travelers to the Blue Bonnet Café, which had moved from Main Street to the highway.

Four

SCHOOLS AND CHURCHES OF MARBLE FALLS

A study of Marble Falls history gives a strong indication that schools and churches have been important to residents since the town's beginning in 1887. In the early days, young children were taught at home or in small groups. Dicie Yett Johnson taught black students in her home.

For older students, Adam R. Johnson and his associates raised funds for a university in their impressive two-story granite building on Broadway. Though that first effort in 1891 did not work out, town citizens kept the building to serve the educational needs of their children. It became the center of the Marble Falls Independent School District, formed in 1908, when students of all ages attended classes there.

Increased enrollment required the construction of a separate high school in 1938, leaving only the elementary students assigned to the first building. Rural schools of the area had closed and consolidated with Marble Falls Independent School District by 1950. When a new elementary school was erected near the granite building in the 1950s, the old site was used only for school administration offices.

Half a century later, increased population in the communities around Marble Falls necessitated the building of new elementary schools in the rural areas of Spicewood and Granite Shoals. School administration offices moved to the north side of town in 2010, and the school board allowed the Falls on the Colorado Museum to move into the historic granite building.

Central Texas College brought college courses to Marble Falls in 1986, holding night classes on the high school campus. In more recent years, Texas Tech University has added upper-level and graduate courses for the convenience of local students.

Several Marble Falls churches had their beginnings when members of rural congregations moved into town. Other churches were organized as the town's residents supported their development. Almost every major church denomination is represented in the town.

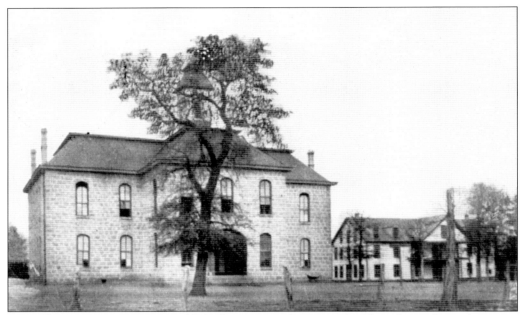

The Alliance University was established in 1891 in the granite building that still stands at 2001 Broadway, near Backbone Creek. Note the tower and the chimneys on the roof. The imposing dormitory building at right was removed from the site before many years had passed. Although the university did not develop, the building itself served the educational needs of the town until 2010. It now houses the Falls on the Colorado Museum. (FOCM.)

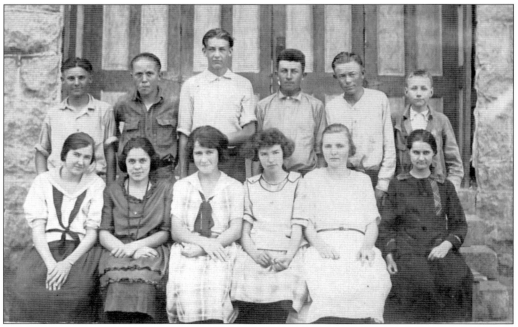

This image of the Marble Falls High School class of 1920 is one of many class photographs that are available for viewing among the displays at the Falls on the Colorado Museum, located at 2001 Broadway (west) in Marble Falls. (FOCM.)

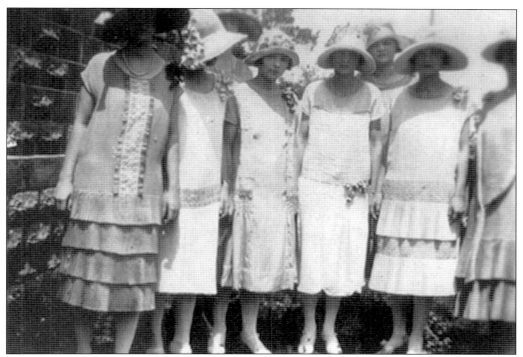

Pictured here are the girls who graduated in 1925 from Marble Falls High School. Helen Ebeling was valedictorian. Other graduates were Beryl Mae Fowler, Birdie Gunn, Viola Herbort, Mary Virginia Lacy, Freda Marie Michel, Phoebe Phillips, and Cleo Smith. (Mary Lucas.)

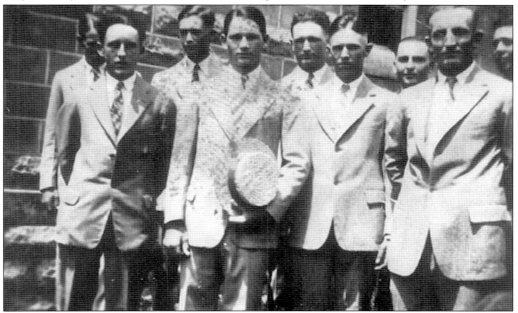

The boys of the Marble Falls High School class of 1925 are shown here in unknown order. They include salutatorian Roy Jones, Porter Askew, Tom Dee Bridges, George Burnam, Hugh Crownover, Herbert Darragh, Charlie Haynes, Tilman Hibler, and Myron Lacy. (Mary Lucas.)

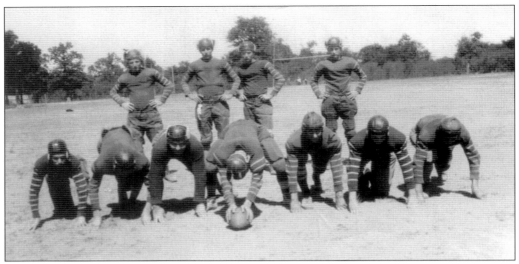

The 1924 Marble Falls football team is seen here. Before their game with the team from Junction was over, Junction lent Marble Falls some players so they could finish the game. Pictured are, from left to right, (first row) Bodie Moore, Charley Haynes, Roy Jones, Alvin Hibler, J.R. Phillips, Hardin Shifflet, and Joe Crownover; (second row) Porter Askew, Tom Bridges, Ben Jarvis, and George Burnam. (Deanna Bradshaw.)

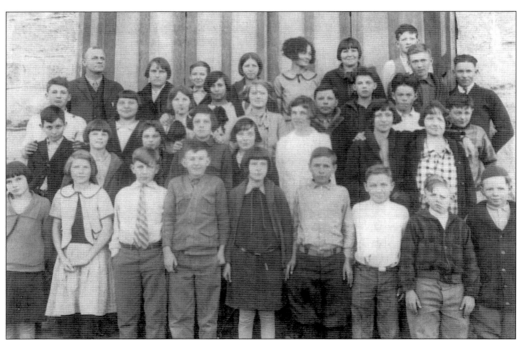

These sixth and seventh graders are pictured on the front steps of the Marble Falls granite school building in the 1930s. Their teacher, John Askew (fourth row, far left) had previously taught at the school in Spicewood. (Jean Eades.)

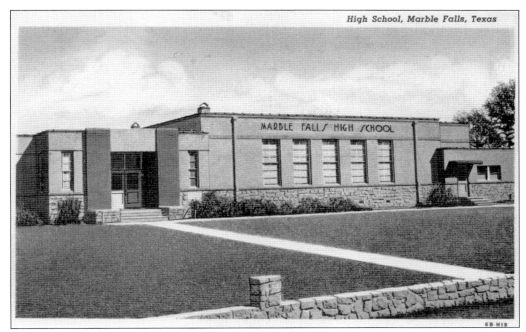

The second Marble Falls High School was located very near the old granite school, but the new structure faced west. Bonds had to be sold in 1938 for completion of the school in 1940. After World War II ended, materials became available to install bleachers at the football field, with a promise of lights for the field soon to follow. (FCCM.)

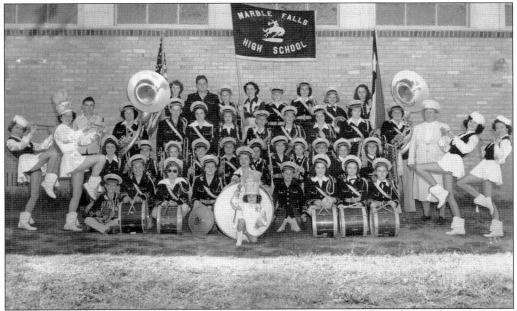

The Marble Falls High School Band was started at the second high school. In 1947, the Lions Club paid for the group's first professionally manufactured band uniforms. The band is pictured wearing their uniforms in 1950, with their director, Vedena Hundley Taylor, also in uniform. Taylor was the director who organized the band. (FOCM.)

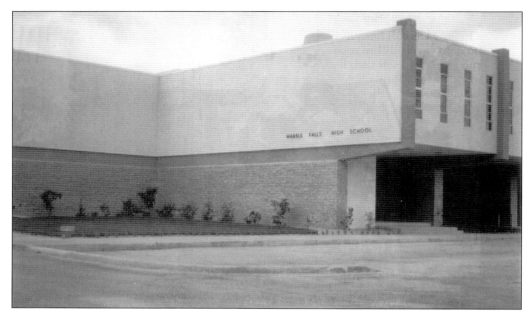

In 1968, classes transferred to the third Marble Falls High School, located at 1511 Pony Circle. With a capacity of 600, the school opened with 256 enrolled. Mustang Stadium, displaying the school colors of purple and gold, was completed in 1970. The facility became Marble Falls Middle School for grades six through eight when the current high school was built.

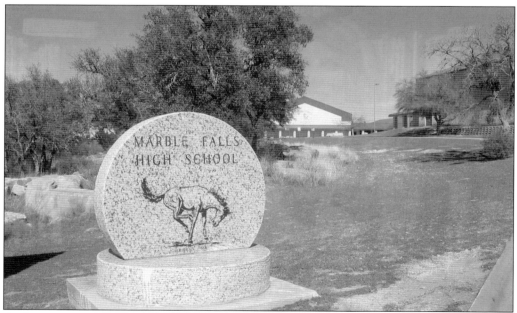

At the entrance to the fourth Marble Falls High School, a granite marker shows the school mascot, the mustang. Campus buildings can be seen to the right. The school is set on a high ridge off Ranch Road 1431 east of town. Farther east, the Manzano Mile is the street that leads to the stadium. Leo Manzano, a 2012 Olympic silver medalist, graduated from Marble Falls High School.

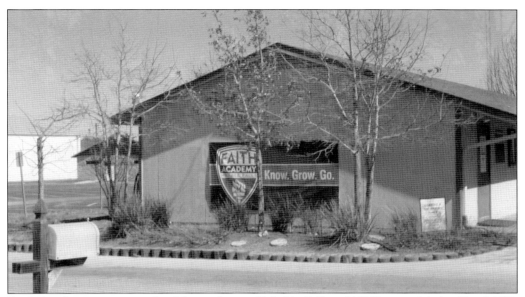

Faith Academy, a private school located east of Marble Falls at 3151 Farm to Market Road 1431, was founded in temporary accommodations in 1999 to serve kindergarten through twelfth grade. Two permanent classroom buildings and a gymnasium now are in use, and all buildings should be completed within the next two years. The high school has 132 students. The sports team is the Flames, and the school colors are red, black, and white. Pictured is a building banner with the motto "Know. Grow. Go."

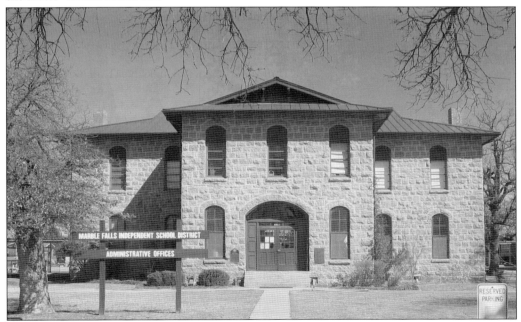

At the time of the old granite school's 100th birthday in 1991, it was being used for Marble Falls Independent School District administrative offices. Charles Hundley was school superintendent. To mark the occasion, former students and town dignitaries gathered to retell the history of the old school and to unveil a historical marker. (Texas Historical Marker.)

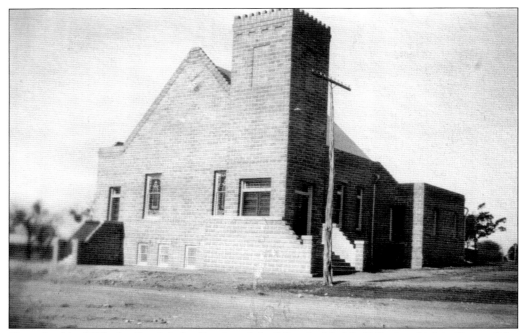

Organized in 1891, the first Methodist church building in Marble Falls faced Main Street. The second church, shown here, was built in 1914 and faced east at the corner of Fifth Street and Highway 281. The second structure included stained glass windows, which were given away when the building was torn down.

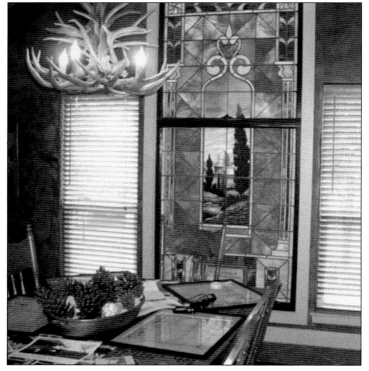

Pictured is the stained glass window given in memory of pioneer pastor Rev. Arter Crownover for the 1914 Methodist church built in Marble Falls. The window is now in the home of a Crownover descendant. Other old windows can be found in private homes and in the Llano museum.

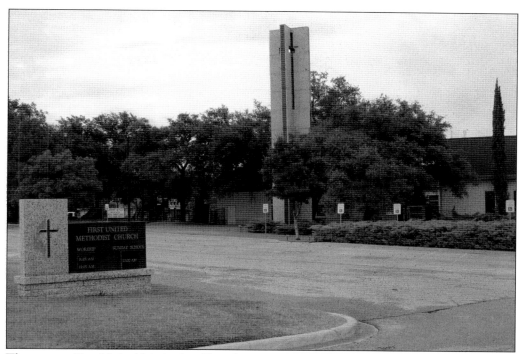

The present First United Methodist Church was consecrated at 1101 Bluebonnet Drive in 1997. Since that time, additional wings have been added to the church.

The First Baptist Church of Marble Falls was organized on September 9, 1888. Before the first building was constructed at Fifth and Main Streets in 1893, services were sometimes held in Johnson Park, where discarded railroad ties served as pews. Rev. Max Copeland moved to Marble Falls in 1958 and was the pastor when a new chapel was built east of Highway 281 in 1961. Later, the church pictured here was built.

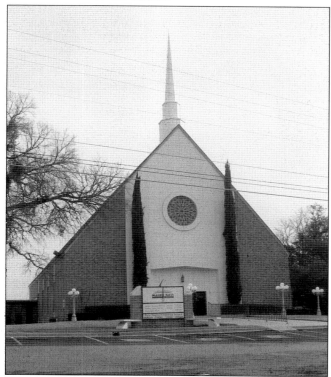

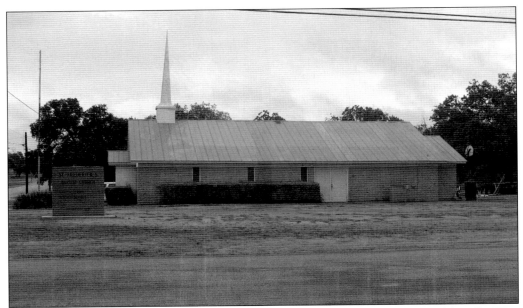

St. Frederick Baptist Church is pictured at 301 Avenue N at Third Street in Marble Falls. This building was dedicated in 1980. The church was founded in 1893, when Dicie Yett Johnson offered her home as a meeting place. Then the church and a school were held in the lower floor of the first Blazing Star Lodge building at Sixth Street and Main before moving to Avenue L near the depot, then on to Avenue N.

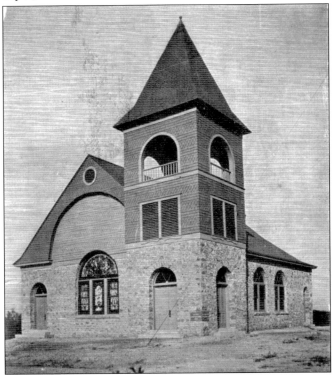

The granite Central Christian Church was dedicated on Main Street in 1908. In 1910, Christmas trees were set up at the Methodist, Baptist, and Christian churches—all located on or near Main Street—with "a cordial invitation extended to everyone" to enjoy the season. In 1955, the First Assembly of God bought the old Central Christian Church building, which now has been replaced.

Pentecostal Church founding pastor Hazel Frusha is pictured standing inside the original church building on Avenue N in the 1950s. Ann Townsend, second from right, stands facing her with other unidentified Bible class students.

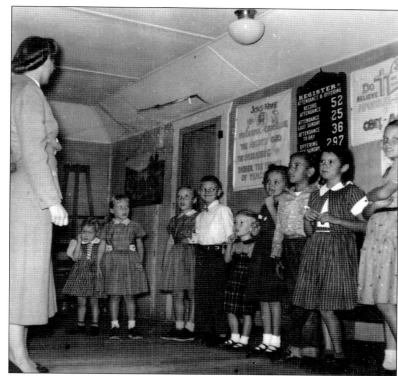

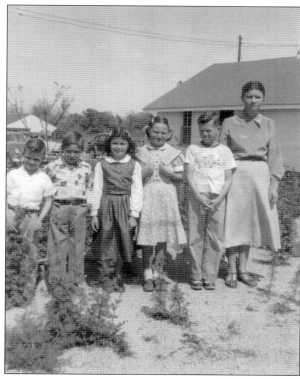

Leona Townsend (far right), a young widow, served as Sunday school teacher for this group of children who attended the Pentecostal church on Avenue N in the 1950s. The children are, from left to right, Roger Wright, unidentified, Townsend's daughter Ann, Reta Maugham, and Townsend's son Earl. (Ann Darragh.)

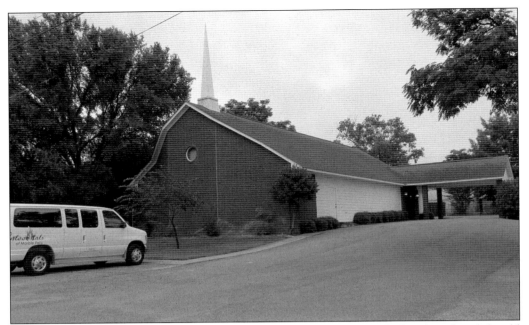

Still located at its original site at 407 Avenue N, the United Pentecostal Church replaced the old buildings with these new facilities.

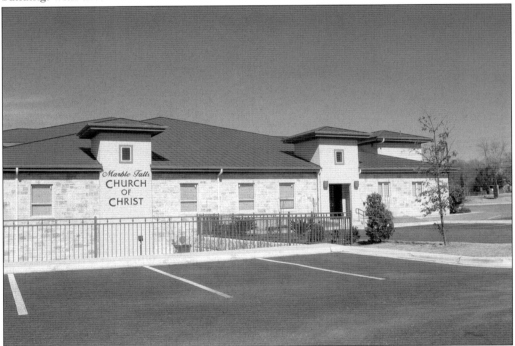

The Marble Falls Church of Christ has been located at 711 Broadway since 1945, when members from Fairland combined with members in Marble Falls. Their first building was moved in from Tobey community. From that beginning, additions were made in 1978, leading to this recently completed building.

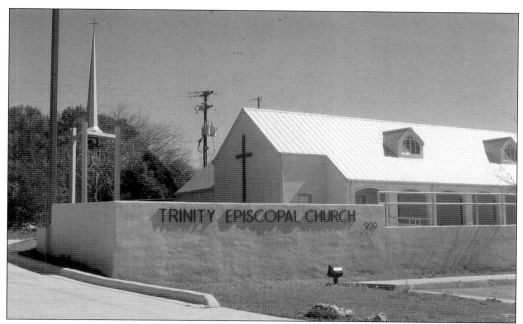

Trinity Episcopal Church is pictured at its location at Avenue D and Ranch Road 1431 in Marble Falls. A few Episcopalians lived in the area as early as 1891 and attended St. Alban's Episcopal Mission, but the present church had its first meeting in Marble Falls in 1954. Members began with a chapel and now have additional buildings.

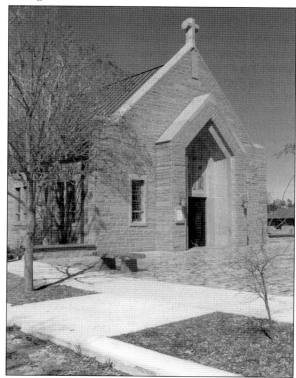

St. John the Evangelist Catholic Church was dedicated in 1961 at 105 Ranch Road 1431 East in Marble Falls. Missionary priests of the Holy Cross Order came to Marble Falls in 1940. In 1954, property for a mission was purchased. By 1957, the Texas Granite Company began construction on the structure pictured here. (Texas Historical Marker.)

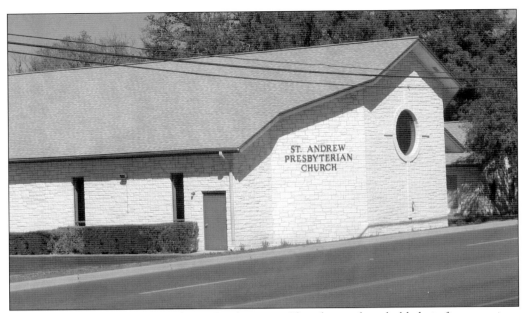

On February 28, 1968, St. Andrew's Presbyterian Church members held their first meetings at various sites around town. They now worship at 201 Ranch Road 1431 East in Marble Falls. J. Arthur Strickland served as their first full-time pastor.

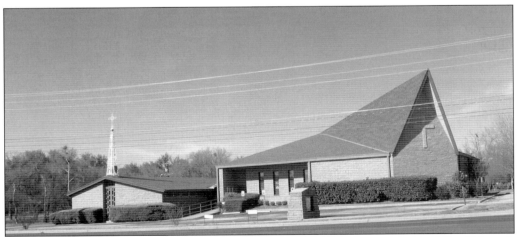

St. Peter's Lutheran Church is located at 1803 Ranch Road 1431 West in Marble Falls. Although many families of the Lutheran faith lived in the area before Marble Falls was founded, the first sanctuary in the town was built in 1962. The church built a new worship space in 1982 and expanded again with more classrooms for St. Peter's Lutheran School for very young children.

Five

MARBLE FALLS IN THE 21ST CENTURY

Marble Falls can be proud of its place in history and of the historical sites that remain as reminders of a colorful past. In addition, residents are able to find employment and answers to most of their other needs within the city limits.

For instance, Historic Main Street in Marble Falls has nine blocks of business sites, restaurants, a library, a theater, and a continuing display of outstanding sculptures. A city-owned area along Lake Marble Falls is an extension of Main Street. It includes a pavilion, a swimming pool, tennis courts, and plenty of space for the annual display of Christmas lights.

The longest-running business in Marble Falls, the Blue Bonnet Café, moved from its 1929 location on Main Street to Highway 281 in 1946. It continues the tradition of serving the local and traveling public.

At the site of the 1894 factory, a new hotel was built in 1999, as were restaurants and office buildings. The Texas Historical Marker that describes the factory has been moved just outside River City Grille, which is near the original factory location.

The granite academy, built in 1891 on Broadway, served Marble Falls schools until 2010. Appropriately, the old structure now is home for the Falls on the Colorado Museum.

US Highway 281 has other businesses, hotels, and restaurants on its eight-mile stretch that runs north and south from the Colorado. In addition, Ranch Road 1431 crosses Highway 281 and stretches from the new Marble Falls High School and stadium on the east side to Granite Mountain on the west side.

In addition to athletic facilities at schools, the community has numerous locations available for sports activities, such as the new soccer fields located along Whitman Creek. The Adam R. Johnson Park provides more space for a ballpark and fishing. It also attracts family reunions, community activities, and an annual boat-racing event. Veterans are honored at two sites in the park and also at centers for veterans' organizations.

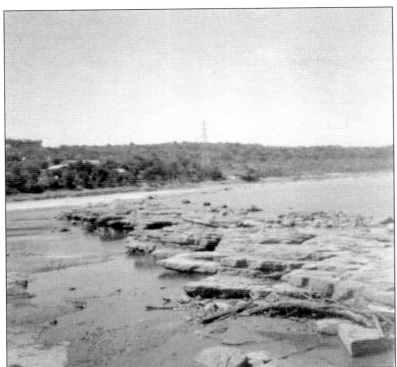

At regular intervals, the Lower Colorado River Authority lowers the water level of Lake Marble Falls for maintenance on private boat-storage structures. When the lake is lowered, the remains of the old falls appear, as shown in this picture. Then, the exposed ledges become an attraction for people who want to experience the thrill of walking across the river as old-timers did.

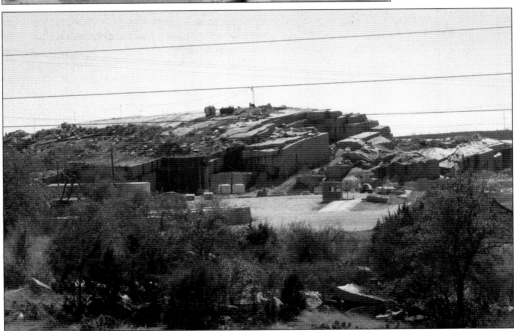

Because Granite Mountain became the center of the pink granite industry that began in the 1880s, this present-day photograph shows a diminished mound of granite. However, a great amount of granite is available below ground at this site. In addition, granite can be found in other locations in the county. (Texas Historical Marker.)

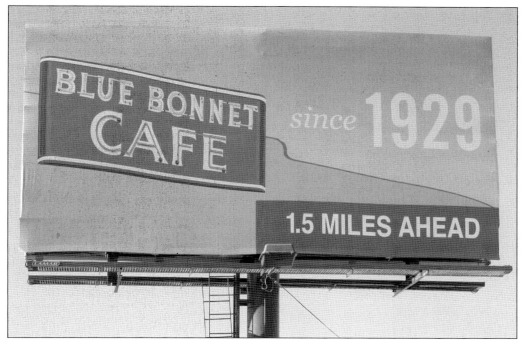

The signs that appear on entrances to Marble Falls remind visitors that the Blue Bonnet Café has been in business since 1929. John and Belinda Kemper purchased it from Don and Flo Bridges in 1981 and upgrade it as needed. It is open every day except for the week between Christmas and New Year's, when the employees have time off to visit with their families.

The historic Blue Bonnet Café was moved from Main Street to this Highway 281 location in 1946. Since opening in 1929, the café has been the go-to place for pie. Photographs displayed inside include those of famous Texans and other well-known visitors who stop to enjoy quality food that is served in an efficient and gracious manner. (John Kemper.)

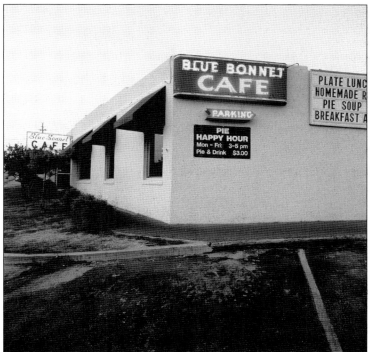

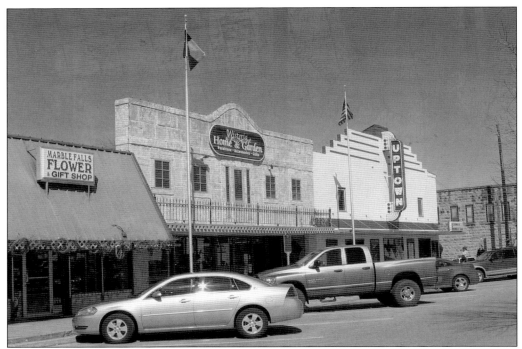

Historic Main Street business owners promote modern hometown services and products along this old street. In front of the Uptown (Marble) Theater, there are footprints made by Astronaut Jim Lovell when he promoted the movie *Apollo 13* in 1995. Parades are held on Main Street, as are chamber of commerce events like Market Days, Lakefest dragboat races, and the December Walkway of Lights along the lake.

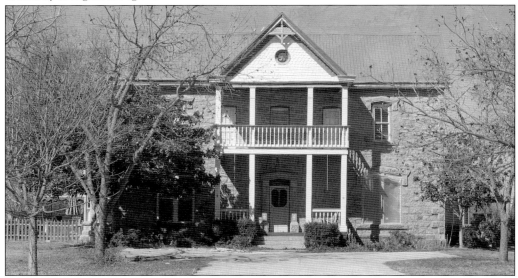

After the Badger family sold this Avenue M granite home in 1943, it had numerous residents until 1965, when Mr. and Mrs. Ray Pinson purchased and restored it. The present owners, attorney Steve Hurst and realtor and city council member Jane Marie Hurst, have made additional major repairs on the aging structure. They now use it as their offices. (Texas Historical Marker.)

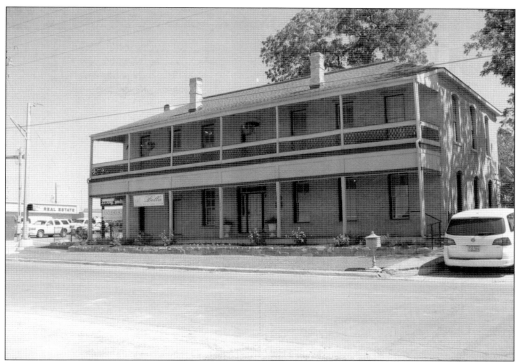

The two-story Roper Hotel is pictured as it appears in modern times. It was built by George and Elizabeth Roper in 1888 when the railroad service became available to Marble Falls. The hotel was purchased by W.F. Smith in 1926, operating as the Central Hotel or the Francis House. His son R.S. Smith and his family ran the hotel in the 1930s. The family sold it in 1963.

Continuing in its original location at the corner of Third Street and Highway 281, the Roper Hotel was restored by Don and Michelle Gunn and opened with a restaurant in the 1980s. In more recent years, it has held offices for realtors and lawyers. Now, it is used as a medical center. It is listed in the National Register of Historic Places, as shown here. (Texas Historical Marker.)

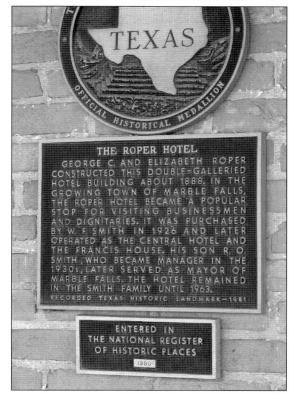

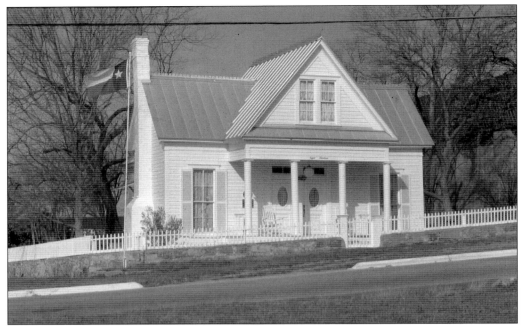

Gov. O.M. Roberts and his wife, Catherine, owned this home in Marble Falls from 1893 to 1896. After the capitol building in Austin burned in 1881, Roberts may have brokered the deal that allowed Marble Falls granite to be used in the construction of the current capitol building. The Roberts home, on Seventh and Main Streets, belongs to a descendant who has restored it. (Texas Historical Marker.)

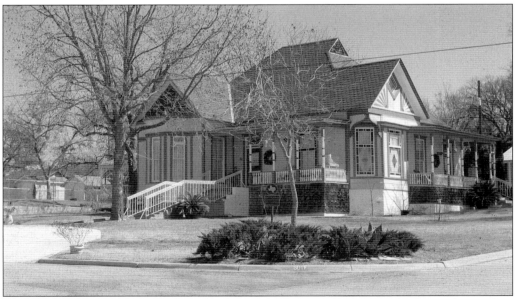

The Otto Ebeling home was built in 1891 on Sixth Street at Avenue F. A banker and a rancher, Ebeling lived in the house with his wife, Emille Giesecke, and their four children until they moved to Austin in 1917. In 1982, his great-nephew Robert Lee Ebeling Jr. and his wife, Jean, restored the Eastlake-style home, which has bay windows with stained glass. (Texas Historical Marker.)

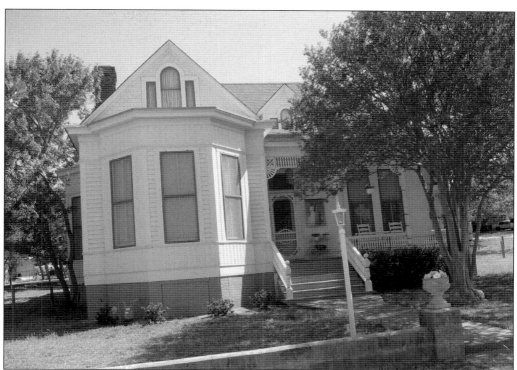

The Christian-Matern House was built in 1892 for Juliet Johnson—daughter of the founder of Marble Falls— who married George Christian in 1887. Present owner Caryl Calsyn restored the building and received a historical marker for it in 1997. She displays photographs of both the Christian family and the Matern family, who owned the home for over 50 years. (Texas Historical Marker.)

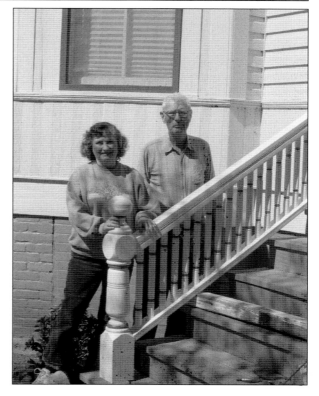

Calsyn is pictured with her brother Dick Duley of Illinois. Because constant care is needed for the old home, Duley helped his sister by making new banisters for the front porch. The Burnet County Historical Commission, United Daughters of the Confederacy, and the Highland Lakes Writers are among the groups that have enjoyed holding meetings at the home in recent years.

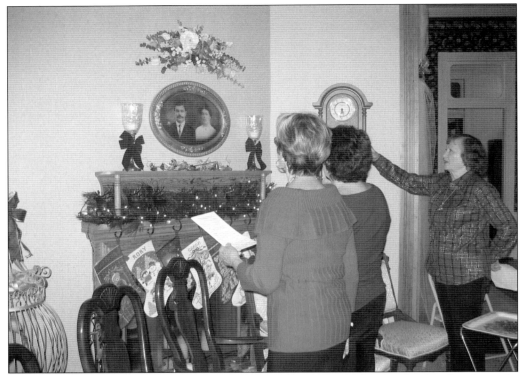

Beginning at Christmas 1999, the board of the Falls on the Colorado Museum has hosted a Victorian open house at the Christian-Matern house. The museum board started the event to thank community members for their support. Calsyn (at right) is shown giving a guided tour of the old home, which still has its three original fireplaces. Following a tour, guests were invited to enjoy refreshments in the festive dining room.

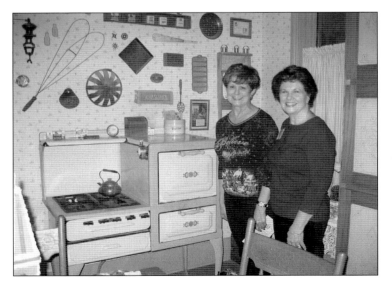

Christmas visitors are pictured with the 1920s stove that is used by the owner of the Christian-Matern house to prepare meals for her family. The oven carries an inscription: Favorite Thermal Oven—Best in the World. It is hard to argue with that when it is still in service after almost 90 years.

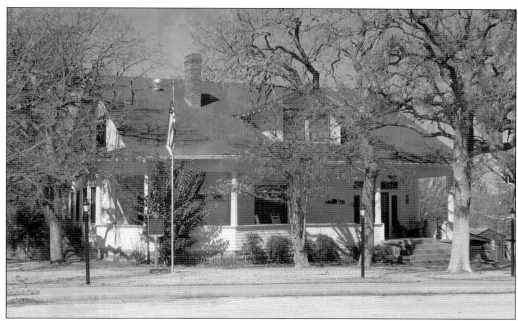

William H. Hoag built this house in 1910. Local rancher Sam Faubion bought it in 1914 and rented it to Alsand J. Fuchs, but it remained in the Faubion family until 1946. Baptist minister Max Copeland and his family purchased it and continue to reside there. (Texas Historical Marker.)

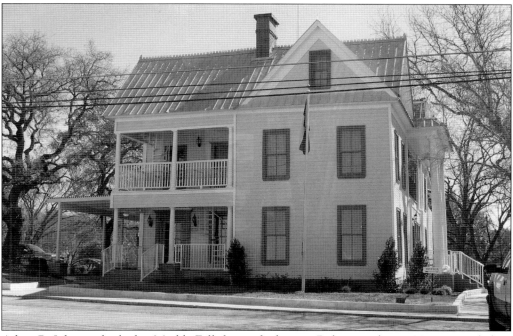

Adam R. Johnson built this Marble Falls house for his son Robert in about 1900. Located close to the south end of the Colorado River bridge, the house was owned at one time by Dr. and Mrs. George Harwood. Beginning in 1946, the Bill Wall family used it as a home and as a bed-and-breakfast site known as Liberty Hall. Since 2006, it has been an office complex.

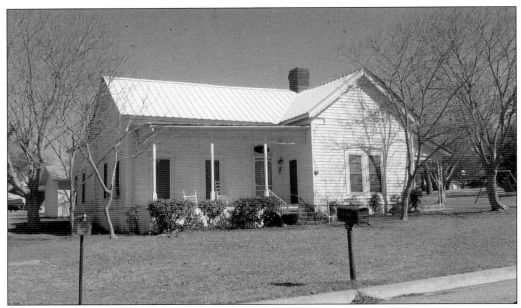

The yellow Victorian house at 511 Seventh Street in Marble Falls was built around 1900. Matilda Faubion was an early owner of the seven-room house, followed by Walter and Viola Cox in 1924. Walter was a barber on Main Street, and Viola was a teacher who had trained at Coronel Institute in San Marcos. The Tommy Allison family has owned the house since 1982.

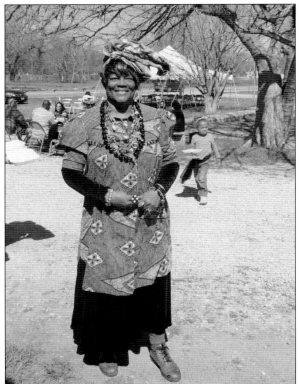

Bessie Jackson is pictured in costume to mark February as Black History Month at St. Frederick Church in Marble Falls. She received the 2012 Outstanding Citizen Award at the chamber of commerce banquet for her work in the outreach program of her church. Jackson served on the Granite Shoals City Council and helped organize the Falls on the Colorado Museum.

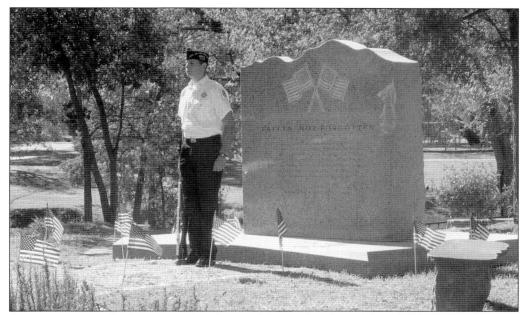

A sentry is pictured at his post at the Veterans Memorial in Gen. Adam R. Johnson Park during the annual Veterans Day commemoration on November 11, 2012. The memorial marker with flagpole and the event are sponsored by the Noon Rotary Club of Marble Falls.

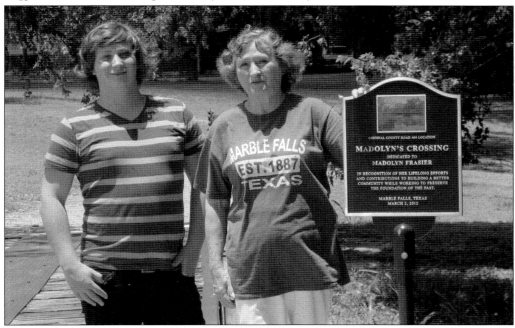

The Gridiron bridge is now set on a walking trail in Adam R. Johnson Park in Marble Falls. County Judge Donna Klaeger and Mayor George Russell participated in a ceremony to open "Madolyn's Crossing" on March 2, 2012, in memory of the late historian Madolyn Frasier. Shown on the bridge are Burnet County Historical Commission chair Caryl Calsyn, right, and her grandson Brandon.

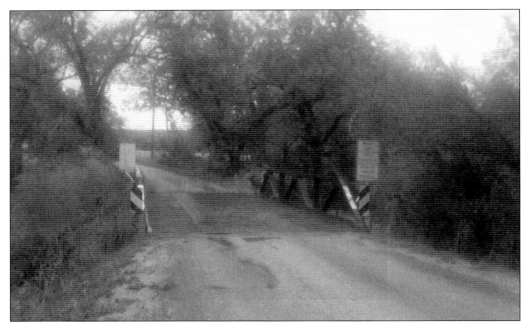

The Gridiron Bridge, built in 1939, is shown in its original location on CR 404 between Marble Falls and Spicewood. It provided a one-lane crossing of the Gridiron Branch of Double Horn Creek and was replaced in March 2012 with a reinforced concrete bridge. (Teri Freitag.)

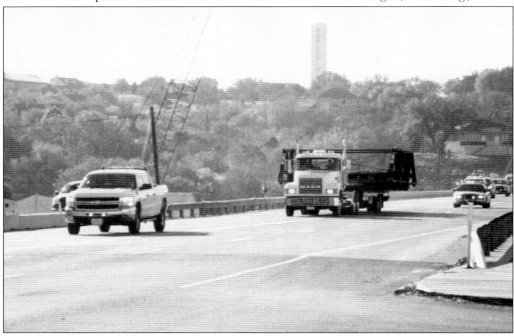

Here, a truck with escort carries the Gridiron Bridge across the bridge over the Colorado River on its way to Johnson Park. The bridge is a Pony Truss–style bridge, with iron high-built siding and sturdy foundation. County Commissioner Joe Don Dockery organized the moving of the bridge and the ceremony in Johnson Park. (Teri Freitag.)

John Arthur Martinez of Marble Falls began work as a country music artist in 1998. A former teacher, his musical career took a real upturn when he won second place on the USA Network talent show *Nashville Star*. He continues to perform and record country music and appears regularly around Marble Falls, often supporting events in his community. (John Arthur Martinez.)

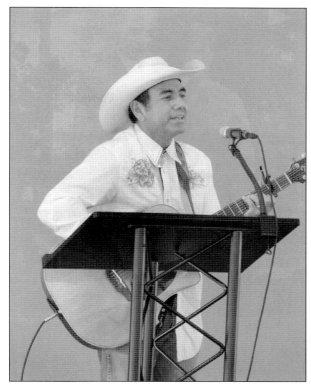

Marble Falls is the focus of major projects that began construction in 2012. In this image, the Colorado River already has one new span carrying northbound traffic. The 1891 bridge was destroyed by a flood in 1935. The second bridge, completed in 1936, has since been replaced by this third bridge. (John Hallowell.)

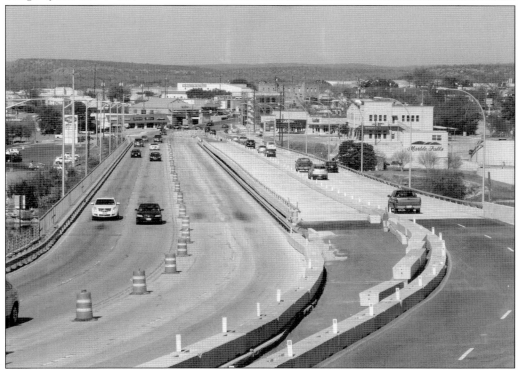

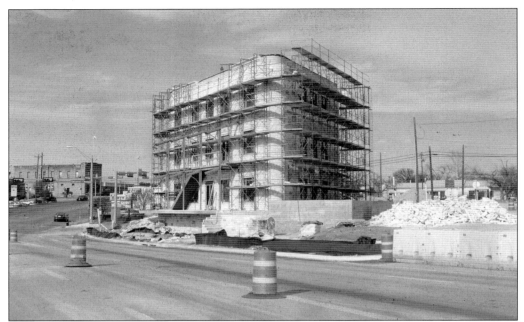

A new visitors center for the Marble Falls/Lake LBJ Chamber of Commerce is shown here under construction near the north end of the Colorado River bridge in Marble Falls. Construction of the white stone, three-story building began on June 1, 2012. The building cost $1.4 million (covered by funds from hotel occupancy tax), and was completed in spring 2013. (John Hallowell.)

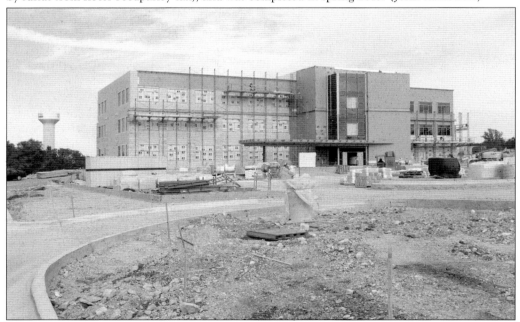

A new Scott & White hospital began to take shape on US Highway 281 at State Highway 71. Its clinic at the Wayne & Eileen Hurd Regional Medical Center set an opening date of June 2013. Construction of a connected 46-bed hospital and a bed tower for 80 beds was set for completion in 2014, bringing the total cost to $150 million. (John Hallowell.)

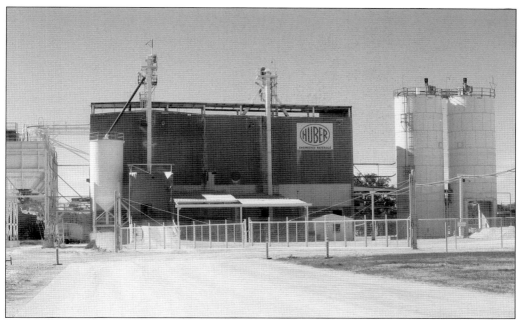

Pictured is the J.M. Huber plant on Avenue N in Marble Falls. Like Granite Mountain, the Huber plant is an important business for the town. V.F. Childers founded Pure Stone Company in 1952 to mine and pulverize limestone. The Huber plant began mining calcium carbonate—a product used in Sheetrock, white paint, and other such products—in the 1970s.

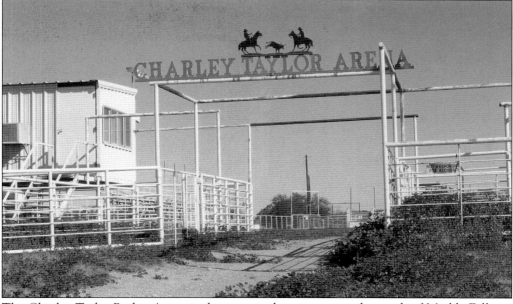

The Charley Taylor Rodeo Arena is shown at its location two miles south of Marble Falls on Highway 281. A parade on Main Street in Marble Falls precedes the summer rodeos. Taylor, with Jack Rogers and Bobby Burnam, created the Marble Falls Rodeo Association and produced the first rodeo in 1958. The first rodeo queen was Arlene Bruns Rhoades, and the first arena was located on Avenue N in Marble Falls.

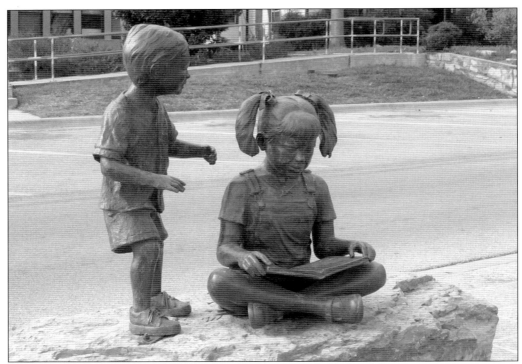

Pictured in front of the Marble Falls Library are figures of two children sculpted by Dan Pogue, who has a gallery and foundry near Marble Falls. Dan and wife Marti Pogue helped develop a juried, year-long display called the Sculpture on Main Street Project. Dan made a sculpture of former Texas governor Dolph Briscoe for the Museum of Western Art in San Antonio.

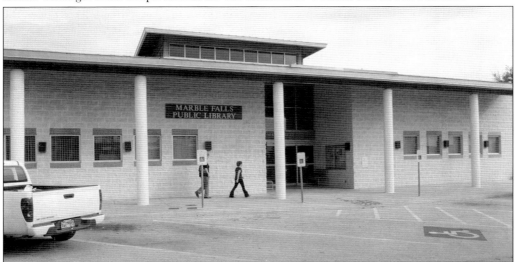

The Marble Falls Library is located at 101 Main Street. It was built in 1997 with funds raised by Friends of the Marble Falls Library Inc and given to the city. The library had previously occupied a smaller, 1974 Friends building at the corner of Fourth Street at Main. Lois Anderson is credited with setting up the town's first library in 1947 in a small area of a lumberyard, then in a downstairs room in the old Masonic Building.

Six

HISTORIC COMMUNITIES NEAR MARBLE FALLS

From the time that Marble Falls was laid out in 1887, rural communities around it were important to the town. The rural settlements needed a market for their products, and Marble Falls needed customers to help it grow. Images of some historic sites and community activities are included here.

South of the Colorado River, Rev. Arter Crownover (1810–1876) and his family settled in the 1850s on the tract of land he had received for service to the Republic of Texas. He and his wife and members of their family are buried in the Comanche Creek Cemetery on that ranchland. Their descendants continue ownership of the land, using Marble Falls for their market and school center.

Also south of the Colorado River, on land granted to the Rev. Adolfus Fuchs family beginning in 1853, the villages of Cottonwood Shores and Horseshoe Bay still have some historic sites remaining from early times. South and east of Marble Falls are several communities that developed before Marble Falls, including Shovel Mountain, Double Horn, and Smithwick from the 1850s and Spicewood from the 1890s.

North of Marble Falls, construction of Backbone Valley's first public building in the Fairland community started in 1859. Finished in 1870, the chapel was named for Rev. Arter Crownover. The building soon also housed a school. The nearby Fairland Cemetery was in use by 1872. In the 1880s, the first loads of granite were hauled by ox-drawn wagons from Granite Mountain to Fairland Depot, then sent by rail to Burnet and on to construction of the capitol in Austin.

Northwest of Marble Falls, Hoover Valley was settled in the 1850s; Tobey, in the 1870s; and Kingsland, in the 1880s. With the development of the lakes came the building of parks by the Works Projects Administration (WPA) during the Depression years of the 1930s. Park Road 4 leads to Longhorn Caverns, developed by the WPA, and beyond to other lakes and parks.

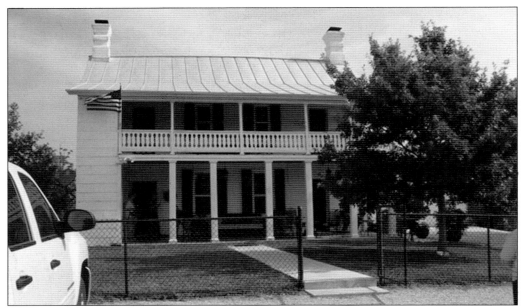

Rev. Arter Crownover and his wife, Levinia Castleman Crownover, built this house on ranchland south of Marble Falls. In 1857, he helped develop the nearby Walnut Creek Methodist Church that continues its regular services. Family members own the house and have added a stained glass window from the Marble Falls Methodist church built in 1914. The window was dedicated to Reverend Crownover.

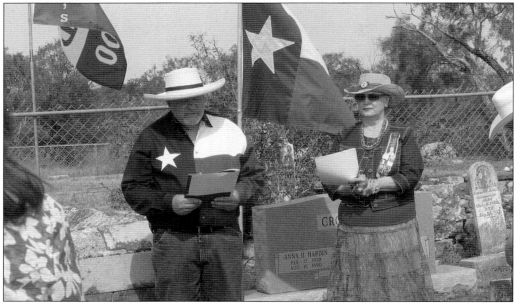

Reverend Crownover, a veteran of the Texas Revolution, and his wife are buried in marked graves in Comanche Creek Cemetery on his ranch. In 2012, special ceremonies honored the Crownovers at the Comanche Creek Cemetery. Nona Hoyer, a Crownover descendant and president of the local chapter of the Daughters of the Republic of Texas, and Buddy Inman, representing the Sons of the Republic of Texas, are pictured. (Texas Historical Marker.)

Murry Burnham is shown in 1954, standing near the second home that his ancestor Jesse Burnam built in the southern Burnet County community of Double Horn. He is displaying his fox kill of the day. Murry and his brother Winston were well known for their Marble Falls store, which carried fishing gear and hunting supplies, including their well-known calling devices that were used to attract wild game. (Murry Burnham.)

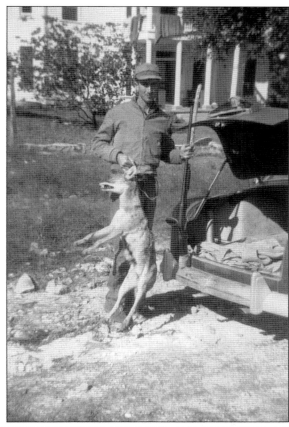

The Burnhams, at home in Double Horn, are pictured with a variety of wildlife killed nearby in 1954. Shown at left is father J. Morton Burnham with his sons Murry (center) and Winston. Murry has written numerous newspaper and magazine articles about hunting and fishing. He and his brother also used to broadcast hunting and fishing news from their Marble Falls store through a San Antonio radio station. (Murry Burnham.)

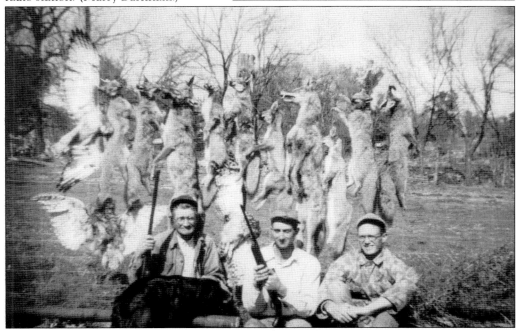

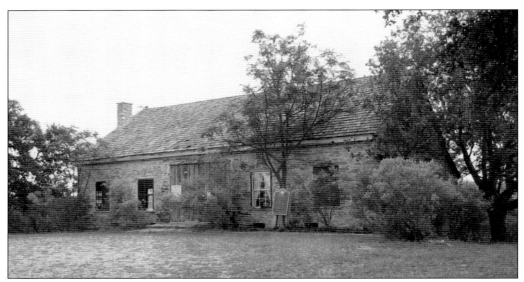

The Conrad Fuchs home was set near the 1870s location of a steam mill at the head of Tiger Creek. The home reflects German building customs. Today it is part of Horseshoe Bay, which became a housing development in the 1970s. Residents of Horseshoe Bay used the old home for Christmas parties and other gatherings for several years, but now the site is in need of repair. (Texas Historical Marker.)

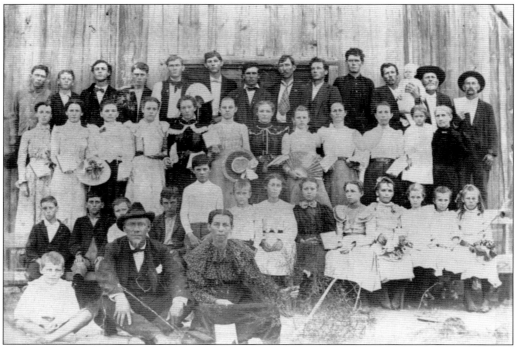

This singing school was held at Double Horn about 1898, with Mr. and Mrs. Copeland as instructors. Events like this, as well as regular church services, were held in the school building or under a nearby brush arbor that was erected for such gatherings. People in the community supported all such activities, regardless of which church was in charge. (Jean Eades.)

Every family had its favorite spot for gathering to exchange news of the day and to picnic along the river or creek. It was the only cool place to be found on a summer day, and it offered younger family members a place to swim while adults prepared a meal that hopefully would include homemade ice cream. (Jean Eades.)

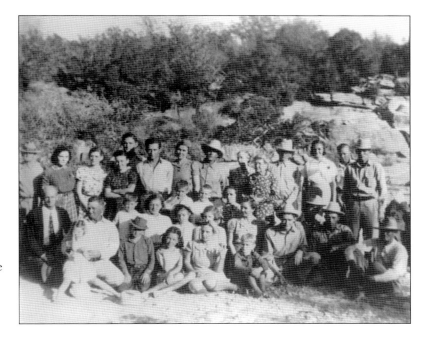

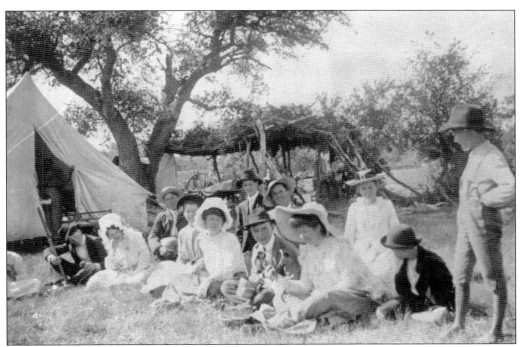

Camp meetings were held for a week or more during the hot summer months at Rockvale. Families came from a wide area, as did church groups from adjoining communities like Round Mountain, Fall Creek, Walnut, and Double Horn. People brought all necessary provisions for their families. Church services were held under a nearby brush arbor. (Jean Eades.)

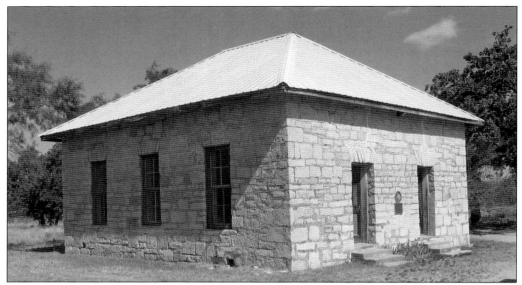

Opened in 1857, Crownover Chapel is located in Fairland, north of Marble Falls, near the Fairland Cemetery. The chapel stands on a seven-acre tract donated in 1859 for the building of a Methodist church and school. Before the structure could be completed, men of the community left to join the Confederate army. The building was finished in 1870 and named after Rev. Arter Crownover, who conducted the first church service. (Texas Historical Marker.)

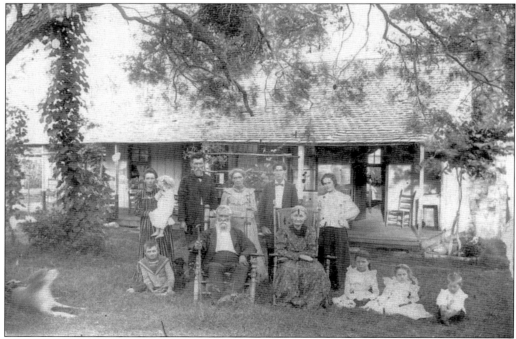

Methodist minister Isaac Hoover and his wife are shown with family members at their home in Hoover's Valley, Burnet County. Hoover's Valley Cemetery, where the oldest marked grave is dated 1854, is located nearby. The graves of the F.M. Whitlock family, killed by Indians in Llano County on December 7, 1870, also are located here. (HB.) (Texas Historical Marker.)

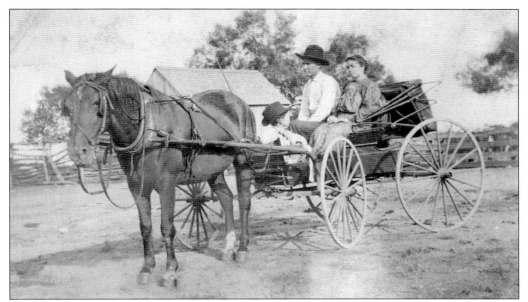

Martin King Jr., son of the founder of Kingsland, is pictured with his wife, Lora Hoover King, and their son Hoover King during a buggy trip to Kingsland in early 1900s. Families in the settlements of Hoover's Valley and Kingsland always had much in common and frequently attended church meetings and family gatherings together. (Willis Springfield.)

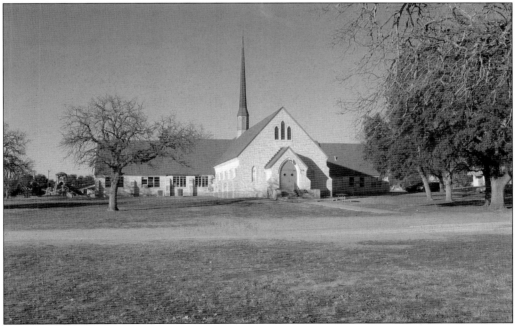

Pictured is the chapel that formerly served the Buckner's Boys Ranch beginning in 1951 on Farm to Market Road 2342. Since 2006, it has served a religious community known as the Smoking for Jesus Ministry. Community members migrated here from New Orleans after their churches and homes were destroyed by Hurricane Katrina. Members have built homes nearby and have set up an elementary school in the old buildings.

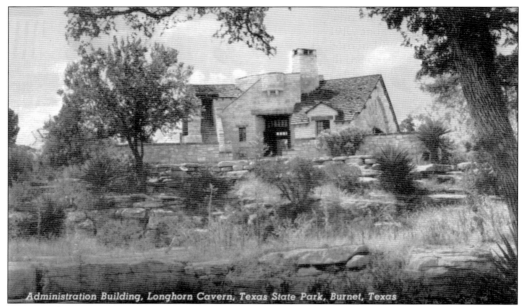

Administration Building, Longhorn Cavern, Texas State Park, Burnet, Texas

From Highway 281, travelers drive along Park Road 4 to reach the Longhorn Cavern Administration Building, shown here, and the actual cavern. The road extends on to Inks Dam. Formerly known as Sherrod's Cave, the cavern was developed by the Texas State Parks Board in the 1930s. As part of Pres. Franklin D. Roosevelt's New Deal, the Civilian Conservation Corps, Company 834, worked in the park. (National Register.) (Texas Historical Marker.)

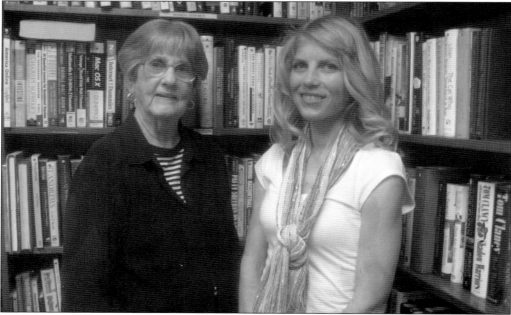

Authors Jane Knapik, at left, and Amanda Rose are pictured in the Marble Falls Library. Rose is assistant director of the library, and Knapik is a frequent user of library resources and a member of Friends of the Marble Falls Library. They support the efforts of library director Mary Jackson as the library moves into the technological future.

BIBLIOGRAPHY

Becker, Billy. *A Pictorial History of Marble Falls: The Land Embracing the Falls on the Colorado.* Marble Falls, TX: *Highlander,* 1999.

Debo, Darrell. *Burnet County History.* 2 vols. Eakin Press, 1979.

Frasier, Madolyn and Mary A. Thompson. *The Valley between the Colorado and the Pedernales.* Nortex Press, 1996.

Goodson, Jim, ed. *Marble Falls, Texas: Celebrating 125 Years.* Marble Falls, TX: *Highlander,* September 2012.

Highlander. 100 Pages of Marble Falls History, 1887–1987. Marble Falls, TX: October 22, 1987.

Marble Falls Messenger. Bridge Dedication Issue, December 11, 1936.

Smithwick, Noah. *The Evolution of a State.* Austin, TX: University of Texas Press, 1983.

www.thc.state.tx.us

DISCOVER THOUSANDS OF LOCAL HISTORY BOOKS FEATURING MILLIONS OF VINTAGE IMAGES

Arcadia Publishing, the leading local history publisher in the United States, is committed to making history accessible and meaningful through publishing books that celebrate and preserve the heritage of America's people and places.

Find more books like this at
www.arcadiapublishing.com

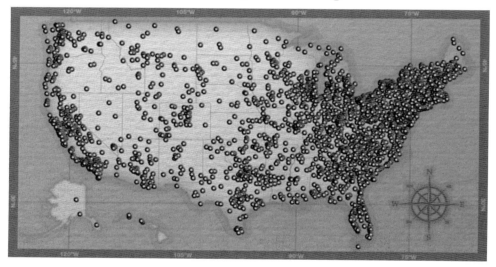

Search for your hometown history, your old stomping grounds, and even your favorite sports team.

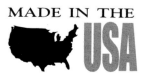